D1648438

Cause Marketing

BUILD YOUR IMAGE AND

BOTTOM LINE THROUGH

SOCIALLY RESPONSIBLE

PARTNERSHIPS, PROGRAMS,

AND EVENTS

Joe Marconi

Dearborn™
Trade Publishing
A **Kaplan Professional** Company

This publication is designed to provide accurate and authoritative information in regard to the subject matter covered. It is sold with the understanding that the publisher is not engaged in rendering legal, accounting, or other professional service. If legal advice or other expert assistance is required, the services of a competent professional should be sought.

Vice President and Publisher: Cynthia A. Zigmund
Editorial Director: Donald J. Hull
Senior Acquisitions Editor: Jean Iversen
Senior Managing Editor: Jack Kiburz
Interior Design: Lucy Jenkins
Cover Design: Design Solutions
Typesetting: Elizabeth Pitts

Portions of Chapter 5, "September 11, 2001," appeared in another form in the November-December 2001 issue of *Interface,* a publication of the American Marketing Association, Chicago, and is used with permission.

© 2002 by by Joe Marconi

Published by Dearborn Trade Publishing, a Kaplan Professional Company

All rights reserved. The text of this publication, or any part thereof, may not be reproduced in any manner whatsoever without written permission from the publisher.

Printed in the United States of America

02 03 04 10 9 8 7 6 5 4 3 2 1

Library of Congress Cataloging-in-Publication Data

Marconi, Joe.
   Cause marketing : build your image and bottom line through socially responsible partnerships, programs, and events / by Joe Marconi.
      p. cm.
Includes bibliographical references and index.
   ISBN 0-7931-5258-5 (6 × 9 hardcover)
1. Social marketing.   I. Title.
   HF5414 .M37 2002
   658.8–dc21

                      2002004699

Dearborn Trade books are available at special quantity discounts to use for sales promotions, employee premiums, or educational purposes. Please call our Special Sales Department to order or for more information, at 800-621-9621, ext. 4410, or e-mail Mindi Rowland at rowland@dearborn.com.

DEDICATION

For Todd and Kristin and Emily
and for Karin

This book about cause marketing appears in print when company policies and practices are being scrutinized more closely than at any time in recent history. This has led to a rich and healthy debate about the role of business in our society, the way business costs and benefits are allocated, and the best way to ensure that business operates for the benefit of everyone.

While there are widely diverging views about how business may benefit and harm local communities and the global economy, there is also a growing consensus that the measure of these impacts must take into account the consequences of not just philanthropy but all business activities. These include the operations of a company and all of its business partners in every part of the world.

Company executives face a daunting challenge as they seek to get their arms around and manage strategically their company's corporate social responsibility activities. As is true for all other business issues of fundamental importance, this means gathering information, setting goals, defining measures, establishing systems for accountability, and assessing progress. In the case of corporate social responsibility, it also means doing this in a way that engages stakeholders and incorporates a commitment to transparency.

As the links between corporate responsibility and business performance become more irrefutable, there is a growing awareness on the part of business leaders that the most effective way to sustain commercial success involves creating corporate cultures that inspire trust and attract support from all key stakeholders. This cannot be done without a thorough consideration of the social, ethical, and environmental consequences of business decisions. These include the following: how capital is acquired and invested; what products and services are offered to the market; where facilities are sited and how they are constructed; who is hired and how these employees are treated; and how a company behaves as a participant in the global marketplace.

All of these traditional business decisions have as much or more to do with how a company affects the community and how it is perceived as do the more traditional investments companies make in providing cash, products, or employee volunteers for community-based charitable organizations.

As companies have begun to understand the potential benefits and costs associated with the full array of their business activities, there has been a dramatic increase in the allocation of funds from marketing budgets that provide some benefit to nonprofit organizations. The expenditure of these funds to serve the interests of both the company and the community has come to be known as *cause marketing*.

When properly planned and executed, cause marketing can benefit a company by boosting sales, increasing market share, and strengthening brand image and loyalty. At the same time, such initiatives also can deliver substantial benefit to the public, including access to new financial support, increased visibility, and new and effective mission-related strategies for specific nonprofit organizations and social causes.

If cause-related marketing is not done well, however, both the community and the company can be damaged. Nonprofit organizations can compromise their purpose, launch initiatives that are not sustainable, and skew their priorities to accommodate business interests. Companies can make investments that do not show a substantial return, help sales or brand image, and even stir up controversies that claim valuable management time.

Effective cause marketing must be viewed by all parties as serving a beneficial purpose. These partnerships must be characterized by integrity and mutual respect. Everyone must share a commitment to clear, timely, and honest communications, and there must be effective mechanisms to address any issues that raise trouble-some questions for any of the collaborators.

A cause marketing initiative alone will not persuade the public that a company is a good corporate citizen. Nor will a campaign that seeks to wrap an otherwise offensive company in a cloak of virtue alter the views of any key stakeholders—except perhaps to make them more cynical.

However, a carefully crafted cause marketing campaign, executed well, can make an important contribution to a company's overall objectives and provide unique benefits to communities where it operates.

This book offers a thoughtful and practical approach to cause-related marketing for large and small enterprises. We at BSR are pleased to have contributed to the content of this book and encour-age readers to take its solid advice to heart—and action.

Robert H. Dunn
CEO, Business for Social Responsibility

C O N T E N T S

No area in business today is more sensitive to the changing tastes and mood of the public as marketing. In each of its various aspects— packaging, positioning, pricing, promotion, distribution, and sales—marketing must achieve a defined business objective and at the same time reflect and respond to what the public says it needs and wants. Accordingly, the marketing process continues to become ever more specialized. A glance at the titles of my previous books will support the claim, as the words *image, brand, shock, crisis, reputation,* and even *future* have been applied to describe various approaches to marketing.

Cause-related marketing has emerged as a powerful method of generating awareness, distinction, affinity—potentially lasting relationships—with members of specific target audiences who have shown a willingness to identify themselves with particular subjects, often emotionally charged.

The anthropologist Margaret Mead said: "Never doubt that a group of thoughtful, committed citizens can change the world; indeed, it's the only thing that ever does."

Over five decades, cause marketing has become a highly visible, often cost-effective, and frequently controversial means of increasing recognition. It has created, enhanced, or changed public perceptions, images, or reputations, and has strongly differentiated individuals, brands, and companies in crowded, competitive fields.

From broad-based global sponsorships and associations, such as United Way, UNICEF, or the U.S. Olympic team, to the support of localized efforts to advance literacy, scholarship, research, health care, environmental issues, or the arts—business, media, and the general public have come to understand the benefits of leading or participating in a cause marketing effort.

This book is first a marketing book for marketing professionals and senior-level managers who need to understand the potential benefits and advantages of cause marketing as well as its potential problems. It is not a commentary on corporate social responsibility, though no doubt some may have crept into this book. In that regard, observations, comments, and conclusions herein reflect the views of the author, based on some three decades in the study and practice of marketing, and do not necessarily reflect the opinions of any of the organizations that contributed information for this book.

More than many other specialized efforts, cause marketing involves virtually every level of an organization from occupants of the executive suite to cafeteria workers, research analysts, and grounds crews. By necessity, some attention must be given to the tested principles of successful marketing on which a cause marketing effort would be developed. These include information analysis, research, and planning.

The cause marketing casebook makes up a significant portion of this work. It includes a varied selection of case studies, some highly detailed and others briefly noted, in an effort to explore how the process has worked—or *not* worked—for organizations of different sizes, and for differing industries, all with dramatically different budgets.

Within the United States and around the world, there is a maturing interest in environmental, ethical, philanthropic, preservationist, conservationist and social issues. Although virtually every issue may be subject to interpretation by the political right, left, or any number of special interest groups, these issues present both opportunities and challenges for marketers and the enterprises they represent.

Cause marketing goes beyond advertising and public relations to focus on essential elements needed to support a socially responsible component of a well-crafted overall marketing plan. The result should build value and add another dimension to a company's or brand's image and reputation by, as experts describe it, *doing well by doing good.*

ACKNOWLEDGMENTS

This book would not have been possible without the generous cooperation of Business for Social Responsibility (BSR), a membership organization for companies seeking to sustain their commercial success in ways that demonstrate respect for ethical values, people, communities, and the environment. Access to BSR's *Cause-Related Marketing: Partnership Guidelines & Case Studies* and to the case studies on ConAgra Foods, Eddie Bauer, Liz Claiborne, Taco Bell, Target, Timberland Company, Ford Motor Company, Grabber Performance Group, Compaq, Mattel, Wal-Mart, and other material was invaluable. The author and publisher wish to express their appreciation to BSR, Dinah Waldsmith, and Lisa Dierkes-Baratta for their thoughtful, painstaking, and generous contributions to this effort.

Thanks also to my new friends at Dearborn Trade Publishing, Cynthia Zigmund and Jean Iversen. And thanks to Keith Jones, Richard Girod, Lonny Bernardi, Guy Kendler, and Karin Gottschalk Marconi for holding the project (and its author) together.

1

Understanding Cause
Marketing

"It is better to give than to receive" is an expression that has evolved from a biblical quotation into a highly sophisticated strategy of modern life and business. That simple reference to the virtue of charity carries a variety of implications and associations in today's world. To some people, the issue is one of basic kindness and generosity. To others, it is a matter of social responsibility—an arguably subjective point that maintains individuals and businesses have an obligation to help care for the planet and one another.

But to a growing number of individuals, companies, and organizations, *giving* is a powerful tool to be used in a calculated program of public relations and long-term investing.

Although kindness and social responsibility suggest a goodness that perhaps rises to the level of nobility, giving for largely PR purposes infers a strategy that might be labeled dishonest—or even sneaky.

In the early part of the 21st century, an era characterized by "spin control" applied to many major events—managing information and influencing public opinion by emphasizing some facts and deemphasizing others—fewer issues seem simple or truly black and white anymore. Most subjects are presented as open to interpretation. Motives are questioned and doing the right thing is often considered a matter of opinion. The simple becomes complicated when

1

the right thing becomes, like beauty, determined in the eye of the beholder.

The 1970s marked a period of social upheaval in the United States and many other parts of the world. The decade that followed preached "greed is good" and challenged traditional values. By the 1990s, companies were learning that their images and the public's perception of them did indeed matter. Good corporate citizenship was rewarded with consumer loyalty and *good word-of-mouth*, a term implying community approval. The phrase *to do well by doing good* became almost a mantra describing both the means and the ends. And more companies were catching on.

BUSINESS FOR SOCIAL RESPONSIBILITY (BSR) AND THE CASE FOR CAUSE MARKETING

Business for Social Responsibility (BSR), founded in 1992, is a membership organization made up of companies seeking to sustain their commercial success in ways that demonstrate respect for ethical values, people, communities, and the environment. Through socially responsible business policies and practices, companies create value for investors, customers, employees, local communities, and other stakeholders.

What began with some 50 participating members in 1992—companies such as Ben & Jerry's, Patagonia, and Tom's of Maine—has grown to include more than 1,400 member and affiliated companies around the world.

BSR functions as a resource for its members, helping companies address corporate responsibility issues, which doesn't mean simply conforming to laws or addressing issues of equal opportunity or community reinvestment. Such conformance is expected (and required), though some organizations will make a special point of noting it on their letterheads and in press releases, as if their conformance was particularly worthy of merit. It is the greater commitment to a cause or issue that establishes a bond with a constituency.

Cause marketing is the action through which a company, a nonprofit organization, or a similar entity markets an image, a product, a service, or a message for mutual benefit.

In the best of situations, a larger, greater public will benefit. As BSR describes what it calls "the new marketing landscape," the organization notes: "Cause-related marketing programs vary in scope and design, in the types of nonprofit partners involved, and in the nature of the relationship between organizations and their marketing partners. In a typical cause-related marketing relationship, a company might donate a portion of each purchase made by customers during a specific period of time to an organization representing a cause or issue. However, not all cause-related campaigns channel money to nonprofit organizations; some engage principally in educational or awareness-building activities.

"Some companies extend their relationship beyond marketing, integrating it with other community involvement activities such as employee volunteerism or corporate philanthropy."

North American companies spent an estimated $630 million on sponsorships related to cause marketing in 1999, an increase of almost 500 percent over the reported 1990 spending. Figures since then have risen substantially.

An Internet search of the phrase *cause marketing* reveals tens of thousands of entries, an indication of how widespread its practice and the interest in it have become.

According to Richard Earle, who drew on a number of sources that included the Advertising Council for his 1999 book *The Art of Cause Marketing,* "Six in ten Americans say they'd buy first from a company that backs a cause they support." Additional research by businesses, trade organizations, and nongovernmental agencies support the claim that cause marketing contributes to increased sales and market share as well as to strengthening a brand's image.

BSR, citing a five-year longitudinal analysis of cause marketing trends by the Roper Organization that was commissioned by the consulting firm Cone Inc., noted that "American consumers and employees consistently support cause-related activities." Further, "Companies can quantify the benefits to their brand, reputation, image, and bottom line." Two-thirds of American consumers report having a greater degree of trust in companies aligned with a social issue; nearly the same number think cause marketing should be standard practice for businesses.

Nine out of ten employees of companies involved in cause marketing programs reported they felt proud of their companies. More than half of all workers said they wished their employers would do more to support social causes, a number that takes on added significance as recruiting costs rise and employee benefits become increasingly important in retaining good workers.

A 1996 Business in the Community qualitative consumer research study conducted by Research International (UK), Ltd., noted the following:

- Eighty-six percent of consumers are more likely to buy a product associated with a cause or issue.

- Eighty-six percent of consumers have a more positive image of a company they believe is doing something to make the world a better place.

- Sixty-four percent of consumers feel companies should make cause-related marketing a part of their standard business practices.

In Business in the Community's 1998 quantitative corporate research survey, again conducted by Research International (UK),

Ltd., the management of the more than 450 companies polled reported overwhelming support for cause marketing initiatives:

- More than 70 percent of chief executives, marketing directors, and community affairs directors believe that cause-related marketing will grow in importance to their organizations in the coming years.

- Seventy-five percent feel cause-related marketing can enhance corporate or brand reputations.

- Eighty-one percent of marketing directors believe that companies should address the social issues of the day.

- Fifty-eight percent of marketing directors agree that a cause-related marketing strategy provides companies with the opportunity to address business objectives and social issues at the same time.

The statistics summarized in these studies not only make a strong case in favor of cause marketing but indicate how far the practice has come from its early days, when only a handful of the largest and most successful businesses in town would take a bow for helping to raise money for *a worthy cause.* That term usually meant a local or national charity that had a high profile in fundraising, such as the March of Dimes, the Community Chest, or Easter Seals. Merchants would collect funds from their customers and pass the contributions along to the charity.

As the population grew, the number of worthy causes increased, constituencies became more focused and segregated, and the benefits to all sides became more apparent. In today's marketplace, the company or organization *not* engaged in some type of cause marketing becomes conspicuous.

An important distinction must be noted, however. Even though cause marketing is about embracing issues, it is not strictly about fundraising or performing charitable works on behalf of worthy causes. Companies that have publicized their channeling portions of their revenue into organizations and funds created to save the rain forests, promote the welfare of animals, or preserve historic sites have inspired numerous other prominent commercial enterprises to become involved and benefit from that involvement and visibility in similar ways.

A company interested in entering into a relationship with an organization strongly identified with an issue or cause—or taking on the management of the cause itself—can pursue a number of strategies and directions, such as:

- Strategic philanthropy

- Sponsorship

- Social investment

- Value partnerships

Benefits to virtually all sides in the relationship can be substantial. But successful cause marketing is more than simply opening the corporate checkbook and instantly becoming the most beloved company in town. In some instances, such attempts have backfired and become embarrassments to companies or have been characterized as being so blatantly transparent in their attempts to "buy" public approval that the companies' reputations were diminished, rather than enhanced, by the experience.

As noted, the expression that has been used most often to define cause marketing—*to do well by doing good*—implies that a company must actually *be* good. The process cannot depend on a single campaign or event to create or change the public's perception of a company. The company must examine its profile and determine if its attributes, policies, procedures, and practices would qualify it to mount a credible effort. If the answer is no, the company might want to put certain procedures or policies in place internally before taking its story to the public.

For example, a company known for having a high degree of employee turnover because of reports (or rumors) that, for whatever reasons, it is not a good place to work will have an uphill battle convincing the public it cares deeply about helping other people through its association with a good cause. A company that is a notorious polluter will not be taken seriously as a partner in an effort to help clean up the environment or the community.

It is necessary for a company to engage in corporate soul searching. If areas of weakness are suspected, revealed, or confirmed, the company must be willing to rethink its corporate philosophy and perhaps reconsider its short-term and long-term goals in order to position itself for success.

BSR identifies ten main topics and areas of importance to business:

1. Corporate social responsibility

2. Business ethics

3. Community investment

4. Community economic development

5. Environment

6. Governance and accountability

7. Human rights

8. Marketplace

9. Workplace

10. Mission, vision, and values

Consider the range and scope these categories encompass.

CORPORATE SOCIAL RESPONSIBILITY

Corporate social responsibility is a large umbrella under which a company must view its overall positioning and determine how its business activities affect employees, the environment, communities, consumers, investors, and other stakeholders—and in what order of priority.

It is not unusual for business leaders to say that their company's number one asset is its people and that without a motivated, well-trained, and well-compensated workforce, the company could not survive, much less compete. Accordingly, companies that put people first are likely to provide excellent working conditions and benefits, such as health insurance, flexible hours, on-site day care for employees' children, family leave, tuition reimbursement, and performance bonuses.

Other companies provide employee benefits according to what the law requires and emphasize that low operating costs and high profits produce a strong return on investment, which in turn fosters growth, expansion, and more jobs for more members of the community. This approach, its advocates insist, rather than day care and flextime, is the essence of a well-managed business and should be its top priority. To be listed by a national magazine or Web site as one of the country's best places to work is considered a charming accolade that makes for good public relations but will likely count for very little when Wall Street analysts begin crunching a company's numbers before offering a recommendation on its stock.

But is being one of the country's best places to work a public relations ploy only, or is there a story behind the story that suggests more than corporate benevolence? Obviously, benefits cost companies money. Studies show, however, that promoting higher employee morale has proved to be a benefit to employers, with recorded increases in productivity, lower rates of absenteeism and turnover, reduced costs in recruiting and training new employees, and fewer on-the-job accidents.

Tom Brown, writing in the *Harvard Management Update,* asked: "Is a company that's good to work for the same thing as a good company? And precisely what does it mean to be a good corporate citizen?" Brown raises a number of broad-ranging questions, such as:

- Is the company fair and even-handed with its policies?

- Is it friendly to families?

- Is it honorably competitive?

- Is it committed to the community?

"People will invariably differ in the relative importance they assign to each," Brown writes, "but the goal . . . is not to achieve a uniformity of opinion on what constitutes socially responsible corporate behavior; it's to encourage individuals to grapple with the issues themselves."

In reality, how much does corporate social responsibility matter in the consideration of a cause marketing program? Isn't it enough to simply do an occasional good deed, such as contribute to the U.S. Olympic team or donate money toward the purchase of a new bus for the local school, and receive credit for it—perhaps a tax deduction and the appreciation of the community in the form of more loyal customers? The answer is that giving is an act of generosity, but *giving by itself* is not marketing—even if the purpose of giving is to make news and attract public notice.

Cause marketing associates a company with an issue, a cause, or an organization that stands for something. A company with a record of apparent dedication to publicity or its bottom line only will find it difficult to establish its credibility with a constituency that believes in, and takes seriously, the principles of a cause, an issue, or a truly committed organization. Corporate social responsibility is about business putting its reputation on the line for something it believes in.

Much of what marketers do is a reflection of the culture at a specific time. It is popular to point out how some individuals and corporations go to great lengths to avoid taking responsibility for their actions. In such a climate, the very concept of encouraging businesses to demonstrate a sense of *corporate social responsibility* seems a challenge; and the term itself is open to interpretation.

BSR regards corporate social responsibility as business decision making linked to ethical values, compliance with legal requirements, and respect for people, communities, and the environment.

In many circles, the term *social responsibility* has become synonymous with do-gooders—people whose sole aim is not only to contribute but at times just to be recognized for contributing. Real social responsibility has, in fact, been shown to produce benefits that can be measured in both quantitative and qualitative terms, as illustrated in a number of studies conducted by major U.S. colleges and universities:

- A DePaul University study concluded that companies with a defined corporate commitment to ethical principles do better financially than companies without such a commitment.

- A Harvard study found that "stakeholder-balanced" companies—that is, companies reflecting the best interests of all groups concerned with how a company conducts its business—experienced four times the growth rate and eight times the employment growth when compared with companies that focused only on meeting the interests of shareholders.

- A University of Southwestern Louisiana study determined that publicity about unethical corporate behavior lowers the stock prices of such publicized companies for a minimum of six months.

- A study by two management professors at Boston College found that companies known for having excellent employee, customer, and community relations were listed among *Fortune* magazine's "most admired companies" more than were corporations known for emphasizing strong returns for shareholders. These distinctions were especially significant in recruiting efforts as well as in dealings with legislators and regulators.

- A 1997 survey of 2,100 MBA students reported that more than half of them said they would accept a lower salary to work for a socially responsible company.

Overall, according to data compiled by BSR, studies have shown that companies appearing on one of the many lists of the best places to work have higher profit margins as well as higher rates of growth and job creation.

Benefits to businesses committed to a known and visible corporate social responsibility position include:

- Improved financial performance

- Reduced operating costs

- Enhanced brand image and reputation

- Increased sales and customer loyalty

- Increased productivity and quality

- Increased ability to attract and retain employees

- Reduced regulatory oversight

- Improved access to capital

Any one of the foregoing considerations provides a compelling argument favoring adoption of a policy that includes a commitment to socially responsible practices. More than a do-gooder position, such a policy makes good business sense.

Avon's market is women. Breast cancer is a leading health concern of women. The partnership of company and cause is logical and credible and sends a message that Avon's concern for women who buy its products is more than cosmetic. (Photo by Karin Gottschalk Marconi)

Recognition of Socially Responsible Companies and Benefits

A tangible indicator of a company's commitment to the greater public good is recognition by a respected industry or corporate group that measures the performance of companies against other companies and confers appropriate honors. One such group, the Center for Responsible Business, each year presented its Corporate Conscience Awards. Although the center itself has discontinued its operations, the awards continue under the management of Social Accountability International, a respected human rights organization. These awards honor "outstanding achievements and pioneering programs in environmental stewardship, employee empowerment and diversity, community partnerships, and global ethics."

Apart from the benefits to each company and organization that delivers evidence of its having a corporate conscience—that is, doing something of measurable value for its people, its industry, its community, and in some instances the entire planet—consider the marketing opportunities that could derive from a dignified reference in ads, press releases, reports to securities analysts, annual reports, sales literature, employee communications, and on business letterheads that the company is a winner of the Corporate Conscience Award for Environmental Stewardship or for Community Involvement.

Some corporate social involvement programs have a better regional fit in areas where local concerns take on greater significance. For example, in areas of extremely high unemployment, programs that create jobs and career opportunities will be more noteworthy. Areas strongly identified with natural or endangered resources may be more concerned with—and receptive to—environmentally focused programs. Marketers need a heightened awareness of the particular or unique concerns of regions, constituents, and stakeholders with whom they would do business.

Other categories for which Social Accountability International confers awards for outstanding achievement include:

- Charitable contributions

- Equal opportunity

- Child labor initiatives

- International human rights

- Global ethics

- International commitment

- Education (literacy)

- Animal rights

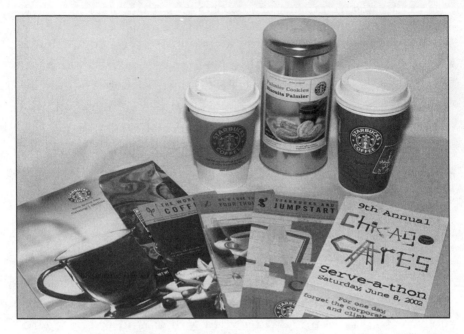

Starbucks supports a variety of causes with a particular emphasis on literacy and education—programs such as Jumpstart—that connect with its core demographic group. (Photo by Karin Gottschalk Marconi)

- Community action

- Responsiveness to employees

- Fair employment

- Family concerns

- Opportunities for people with disabilities

Clearly, some of these categories will raise an eyebrow in at least a few corporate boardrooms. Animal rights, for example, has a huge number of advocates but perhaps as many people who question its being designated a priority among perceived greater priorities. A cause marketing program should reflect the profile and personality of the company and the constituency it strives to serve.

Among the recipients of awards since this organization began presenting them in 1987 are some of the best-known and most respected names in U.S. and international marketing, including:

- General Mills
- Avon Products
- British Airways
- British Petroleum
- Economat
- Dollar General Stores
- Novo Nordisk (Denmark)
- J. Sainsbury (UK)
- Wilkhahn Wilkening (Germany)
- W. K. Kellogg Foundation and the Kellogg Company
- Community Pride Food Stores
- Toys "R" Us
- Sporting Goods Manufacturing Association
- Levi Strauss & Company
- Pfizer

- Starbucks Coffee
- Colgate-Palmolive
- Xerox Corporation
- Shorebank
- S.C. Johnson & Son
- Aveda
- Foldcraft
- Prudential Insurance
- Tom's of Maine
- Time Warner
- Hallmark Cards
- Smith & Hawken
- Ben & Jerry's
- Federal Express
- South Shore Bank
- Johnson & Johnson
- Stonyfield Farm

Of the companies receiving the Corporate Conscience Award, some are well known and some barely known outside their particular industry or region. What they have in common is recognition of the potential value of, and the commitment to, a cause marketing program that puts their reputation behind that commitment. The results in each case were not only positive but judged extraordinary—significant enough to rate being singled out for recognition and an award.

Among many of the better-known companies, there is little commonality in terms of a public image. Some are positioned to the left on the political spectrum, where one might expect to find some of the more high-profile social causes; others are further to the right; and still others cannot be so readily classified. Corporate social responsibility and cause marketing are the instruments of neither liberals nor conservatives and can be appropriately employed by virtually any company, organization, or industry to fit the needs of its marketing plan.

BUSINESS ETHICS

Adhering to business ethics seems a foregone assumption for any company in any business, socially responsible or not. Could any company expect to remain for long in the marketplace if it were regarded as unethical? Has any business ever openly appeared indifferent to questions of ethics? Would a company that was perceived as unethical be likely to enter into a cause-related marketing effort anyway?

The obvious answer to all these questions is no, and yet each year brings fresh reports of the ethics of a major company or its management being called into question. Business ethics defines how a company integrates core values, such as honesty, trust, respect, and fairness into its policies, practices, and decision making, according to BSR's definition.

A 1999 survey of consumers in 23 countries revealed that more than one-third of the consumers in 15 countries surveyed believed it was important that larger companies in a society "set higher ethical standards and help build a better society." The survey was the work of Environics International, the Prince of Wales Business Leaders Forum, and The Conference Board, highly respected research organizations. The same report noted that 40 percent of the surveyed consumers had considered punishing a company based on its low ethical standards. The math here is easy: When a combined total of some 60 percent of consumers across 23 countries regard a company negatively, that company has problems.

Developing and committing to a defined policy on business ethics sends a message to a company's employees, its industry, its investors, the governments that regulate it, and the public that the company has given the issue some serious consideration and wants to be "on the record" with its policy.

Levi Strauss, makers of Levi's jeans and other products, regards business ethics as an important consideration in the marketing of its products as well as in the marketing of its corporate image. While insisting it will "always be mindful of our promise to shareholders that we will achieve responsible commercial success," the company offered the six ethical principles it uses to guide its business: *honesty, promise keeping, fairness, respect for others, compassion,* and *integrity.*

The outline of its ethics policy should typically include a company's position on competitive conduct, conflicts of interest, and corporate values. Before taking a stand and relying on your good reputation to count in the marketplace, you should carefully consider what has deliberately formed the basis of that reputation and evaluate how the company is measuring up against it.

COMMUNITY INVESTMENT

Community investment can encompass a broad range of activities, from supporting a local adopt-a-highway program or blood drive to sponsoring a regional musical arts program. Each company must first determine how it defines its constituent community. For some businesses, community is defined as current, former, and prospective customers; to others, it is the global village accessible via Internet and satellite communications.

If a company is new to the community, whether just moving into a particular location, starting in business, or going national or global, a cause marketing partnership can be a shortcut to greater visibility and a means of defining the company's positions to its target audience.

If a company is well established in a location, a cause marketing program allows the company to position (or reposition) itself by giving something back to the community that helped it to grow and succeed, even if that community is the world.

One of the strongest components of community involvement is the use of volunteers. Employees who volunteer their time to a cause offer multiple benefits. To the volunteer employees, it is a chance to develop relationships within the community and find satisfaction in helping those who may be less fortunate. Employers who create ways of rewarding or acknowledging the work of their employees benefit by (1) giving to the community in the company's name; (2) enhancing the company's reputation as both a good employer and a good corporate citizen; (3) opening multiple opportunities through signage, stickers, buttons, and clothing, along with photos and press releases to raise awareness of both the cause and the company in a positive way at a minimal cost; and (4) doing something worthwhile that will be good for employees, local citizens, and the company.

Even online to a global audience, companies are finding ways of promoting a sense of community. Donations of products and services, matching contributions of employees and/or customers to a cause, and paying employees their normal wages for a certain number of hours per week or per month that they devote to advancing the goals of the cause are some of the ways community involvement can be promoted.

COMMUNITY ECONOMIC DEVELOPMENT

Community economic development is an area that dramatically exemplifies ways in which cause marketing is much more than events or fundraising campaigns. A business that employees underutilized workers in a community—seniors, students, minorities, handicapped people, for example—is championing the cause of fair employment, tapping a pool of workers that fall outside many posted job descriptions, and investing in the financial health of the community. Although almost everyone has acknowledged that fair employment is both legally and morally the right thing to do, realistically many businesses have set the bar in terms of educational and experience requirements that systematically exclude many willing, needy, and capable workers. The best places to work typically and consciously do not.

Community development banking includes providing loans for homes and businesses in particularly depressed communities, supporting the establishment of new dealerships or franchises in such communities, and recruiting and retaining typically underutilized workers. These are some examples of community economic development as cause marketing.

ENVIRONMENT

The word *environment* speaks volumes in the imagery it invites. It also provides a wide platform for staging meaningful cause marketing efforts. Although what is ultimately in the best interests of the environment has become a subjective and often controversial matter, a business pursuing this area of interest can find issues to embrace at several levels.

Concern for the environment is (or should be) universal. How that concern is expressed and channeled into what a company determines as its socially responsible position is for each individual company to decide. BSR's *Cause-Related Marketing: Partnership Guidelines & Case Studies* offers environment-related topics that include:

- Alternative energy sources

- Energy efficiency

- "Forest-friendly" practices

- Green building design

- Green product design

- Waste reduction

- Water conservation

- Water quality

The fact that the subject area is so broad allows businesses the opportunity to adopt an environmental issue with an element of uniqueness in each situation. Indeed, such a strategy is recommended. Even though certain products may be labeled "environmentally friendly," the most successful cause marketing programs focus on more specific aspects, such as donating a designated portion of the proceeds from each sale of a product to a fund to save the rain forests, clean up Lake Erie, establish a wildlife preserve, or underwrite research on global warming. The "green movement" grew out of widespread efforts to publicize and promote products that did no harm to the environment, most typically products that were recyclable, biodegradable, and/or nonpolluting. Earth Day was established to focus on green and environmental issues.

The two most compelling reasons why a business would embrace, and enter into, a cause marketing program relating to environmental issues:

1. To do so infers a strong sense of corporate social responsibility.

2. The issue, in virtually every one of its various forms, has a vast worldwide constituency that looks favorably on businesses that are proenvironment and unfavorably on businesses that are not.

GOVERNANCE AND ACCOUNTABILITY

Governance and accountability appear to be dry housekeeping items—internal matters of little interest to anyone other than a company's board of directors, stock analysts, and shareholders. But the management of a company both sets the tone and speaks for the company. The public image of people elected or appointed to positions on a board of directors, executive committee, advisory group, or management team can have a significant impact on public and stakeholders' perceptions of what a company stands for and what direction it is likely to take. The appointment of a CEO with a past history inconsistent with the stated mission of, or causes most closely identified with, a company can create confusion about what that company represents and the seriousness of its commitment to a cause.

HUMAN RIGHTS

Human rights is an issue that attracts considerable media interest, though normally in the context of international politics and law. At the corporate level, businesses of virtually any size can be judged for their position on human rights as applied to discrimination, codes of conduct, wages, health and safety concerns, working conditions, fair employment practices, and representation. A business that would choose to identify itself with a fund or cause committed to working for human rights in countries around the world and at the same time turn a blind eye to such issues as fairness and discrimination within its own organization not only undermines the cause in relation to marketing issues but invites a legal and public relations problem closer to home.

It can also be assumed that an organization's becoming involved in a cause marketing effort as a way of raising its public visibility and awareness will attract a higher level of scrutiny than a company that chooses to keep a lower profile. A history of employee, industry, or public grievances is likely to be uncovered if it exists and invite charges of hypocrisy.

In perhaps no area of business is the phrase *attempting to look good* as important as it is when presuming to speak on behalf of an issue such as human rights.

MARKETPLACE ISSUES

Marketplace issues typically include many of the areas traditionally associated with marketing, such as advertising, customer service, product development, pricing, and certainly cause-related marketing itself. Increasingly, *consumer privacy* has emerged as an important issue in the marketplace, particularly as the growth of both market research and Internet business has resulted in more information being accumulated in databases and more data being routinely sold in the form of mailing lists and demographic reports. The explosion within the field of telemarketing would not have been possible without the availability of information now being generated and, with that, complaints of intrusions and compromises regarding the privacy of consumer data.

Ethical and corporate social responsibility becomes increasingly important as the marketplace becomes more crowded and competitively intense and as information is moved with unprecedented speed. In a crowded, competitive environment, gaining access to a qualified target market group before the characteristics of that market begin to shift is a priority and supports the creation of cause marketing efforts.

WORKPLACE ISSUES

Workplace issues focus on such areas such as fair compensation, benefits, diversity, recruitment, training, and maintaining working conditions that promote a safe and healthy job environment. Again, the company or organization that undertakes some form of cause-related marketing invites investigation into its workplace activities, history, and practices and its organizational structure. Issues such as health and safety take on added importance. Lawsuits or grievances involving charges of discrimination on the basis of race, age, or gender, or allegations of harassment come under scrutiny and are weighed against a company's claim that its aim is to do good. Situations revealed to be transparently hypocritical serve only to damage a company's reputation despite its noble announced intentions.

MISSION, VISION, AND VALUES

The mission, vision, and values an organization espouses serve to identify it and define it in the workplace, in the marketplace, and among various constituent groups, such as shareholders, regulators, and the media. A decision to support or lead a cause marketing effort can greatly accelerate awareness of a company within such constituencies, but it also creates a degree of transparency that reveals whether the company's principles are consistent with its commitment to the designated cause. A company that has acknowledged inconsistencies and is less than open to inquiry and scrutiny will find unwelcome the attention that accompanies identification with a high-profile cause.

A mission statement and a representation of its values tell the marketplace what the company stands for, but the company must be supported by a record of actions that confirm such representations. Each of these key elements of mission, vision, and values, separately and together, is important to mounting or participating in a successful cause marketing effort. Being a "good" company— serious about corporate social responsibility and business ethics in the workplace and marketplace—is essential. This is true whether the cause is local, national, or global and whether the focus is corporate philanthropy on a grand scale or championing an issue that will change lives, and often also change how people perceive the company.

Business for Social Responsibility notes that some companies extend their relationships with organizations beyond marketing, integrating it with other company activities such as employee volunteerism and community involvement on a large scale. Being a "good" company as well as a concerned, corporate and socially responsible, and ethical employer is not cause marketing. But it is doubtful whether a successful effort in cause marketing can provide a lasting measurable benefit (to the company or the public) if such attributes are not present.

It is not the responsibility or obligation of all business owners or organizations to embrace an issue or cause. But it is becoming more and more common for them to do so; and research overwhelmingly indicates that the public looks more favorably on those that do. Many people believe it is everyone's obligation to give something back to the community, whereas others refuse to accept that belief as an obligation.

To work on behalf of socially responsible issues and contribute time, money, and visible support to a cause that invites approval from the public and especially from a specific, desired target market is simply good for business.

S U M M A R Y

- Cause marketing is the means through which a company, a nonprofit organization, or a similar entity markets an image, product, service, or message for mutual benefits.

- A company might donate a percentage of its profits to support an issue or cause, or it might engage in educational or awareness-building activities.

- Sixty percent of Americans surveyed said they would buy first from a company that backs a cause they support.

- About two-thirds of Americans have a greater degree of trust in companies aligned with social issues.

- Ninety percent of employees of companies involved in a cause marketing program say they feel proud of their association with the company.

- Cause marketing can be carried out in a number of ways, including strategic philanthropy, sponsorship, social investment, and value partnerships.

- Before undertaking a cause marketing program, a company should first commit to being a "good company" and have a clear position on the topics and areas of importance to business: *corporate social responsibility, business ethics, community in-*

volvement, economic development, the environment, governance and accountability, human rights, marketplace and workplace issues, a mission, a vision, and *values.*

- Cause marketing joins a company with an issue, a cause, or an organization that stands for something.

- Corporate social responsibility is decision making linked to ethical values, compliance with legal requirements, and respect for people, community, and the environment.

2

When the Cause Fits
the Company

The company or organization has made a decision to go ahead
with a cause marketing effort. Now what?

The world seemed a much simpler place a few decades ago, and
such a decision might have been carried out with relative ease. For
example, employers agreed to withhold an amount from employees' paychecks, match it with a corporate contribution, and write
one fat check for the total amount to United Way, a group of worthy
charities that funded any number of good causes and activities in
hundreds of communities. Then the employer would receive a letter of thanks from the head of United Way, frame and hang the letter in the public reception area, and publicize its generosity in
press releases, ads, mailings, employee newsletters, and elsewhere,
making certain that the company received credit for its good deed.
Everybody looked good, felt good, and was proud.

But much has changed since those simple days. Even in times of
peace, the world seems a chaotic place, and no one seems quite
sure whom to trust anymore. A person writing a check to help
someone in need stops to wonder if that check will ever actually
reach that someone or if it will end up buying a corporate yacht.
With all due respect to Barbra Streisand, people who need people
are no longer the luckiest people in the world. In 1992, scandal
rocked United Way when its chief executive was accused of finan-

cial misconduct and replaced in an extremely public airing of the organization's dirty laundry. Many employees who had contributed for years felt as if they had been defrauded. Many employers were also angry and were criticized for not keeping a closer eye on where the money went.

A reorganized United Way spent a decade attempting to regain public trust and restore its reputation with some, but not complete, success. Other organizations were subjected to greater scrutiny, and some businesses reconsidered whether such well-intentioned partnerships might not be too potentially risky, concluding that perhaps business should stick to business and stay out of the "helping people" industry.

The climate was changing for many charitable organizations as well. For example, companies once willingly agreed to serve as drop-off points—positioning large collection boxes at their entry ways—to participate in the U.S. Marine Corps' annual Toys for Tots campaign that collected toys for distribution to underprivileged children at Christmas time. It was a great "feel good" holiday event for the companies. The Marines showed a lot of "heart" and proved that members of the corps were more than a superb fighting machine. They and participating companies were helping to bring joy to children. For the small price of a toy, people could make a child smile. Everybody won. The whole arrangement looked and felt great—a cause that seemed individual and personal yet big enough to go around. Then the press conferences and lawsuits started.

Charges began flying that many of the toys were deemed unsafe by changing standards and would have to be disposed of. Drop-off points at many locations took up valuable space and were often said to be obstructing exits and posing risks to safety. Many of the boxes were relocated to local firehouses with visibility of the campaign greatly reduced. It didn't feel good anymore.

In addition, a variety of other worthy causes, from food pantries to feeding homeless families, "mitten trees," the Make-a-Wish Foundation, the Starlight Foundation, the Special Olympics, and a myriad of other heartwarming causes began appearing on the scene with great fanfare, creating competition to make children smile. Toys for Tots, still a well-conceived and worthy concept, was overshadowed and seemed dated in comparison with many of the newer entries. Competition among charities could be ferocious at times.

And how tough was the simple act of buying a toy becoming? Would a child be happy with anything less than one year's toy *du jour*—a computer game, Beanie Baby, Elmo doll? Was Barbie politically incorrect for a wide-eyed little girl?

Cause marketing still seemed like a solid idea for creating goodwill and putting something back into the community, but the many choices of causes with clever trademarked names was only the beginning. What were the potential risks to a company in terms of legal liabilities and possible damage to its reputation if an association with a particular issue or cause received negative publicity? It happens.

The most respected organizations are routinely examined under a media microscope, and mere suspicions are often treated as scandals at the slightest signs of doubt. Disgruntled employees can easily find someone to listen to their complaints, present rumors as "information from an unnamed source," and openly challenge the motives of people who are treated as guilty until proven innocent.

An investigation into reports of serious improprieties surrounding the staging of the Olympic Games in Salt Lake City, Utah, occasioned a long list of "proud sponsors of the U.S. Olympic Team" to be somewhat less than proud of their involvement. In 2001, the American Red Cross was accused of allocating money for purposes other than those for which it had been solicited. The organization changed its leadership and mounted a major campaign to defend its image, thereby making front-page news and becoming the lead stories on the evening TV news shows. Cable news stations repeated the story every half hour.

What had been fundraising efforts of major proportions for noble purposes became an exercise in damage control that left individual and corporate supporters confused, embarrassed, and often angry.

PICKING THE APPROPRIATE CAUSE: IT ONLY LOOKS EASY

The business community and many well-intentioned organizers were beginning to see that a good deal more was needed to support a worthy cause than was apparent or known to the public. Organization and management were huge, frequently awesome undertakings. And the effects of such efforts were sometimes less than companies had hoped, frequently leaving reputations tarnished rather than enhanced.

Where direct charitable payroll deductions and drop-off/pickup collection stations had been simplistically identified with businesses helping to do good deeds for many years, fundraising for causes in recent decades has become more visual and media focused. Marches, walk-a-thons, bike-a-thons, auctions, hikes, rides, concerts, rodeos, athletic events, arts showcases, and much more were the new symbols of charity. Cause marketing had become, if not fully an industry, a field of endeavor in its own right. Advertising and public relations firms created divisions and teams specializing in cause-related and nonprofit programs. Some agencies, in fact, handled nothing else.

Business for Social Responsibility (BSR) notes that "to compete successfully, companies must navigate a complex and constantly changing set of economic, environmental and social challenges and stakeholder demands. Long considered business 'externalities,' such factors are now integral to corporate operations and directly contribute to brand reputation and financial performance."

Consulting firms now specialize in screening and finding partners for such programs, and organizations have been created to manage and market large-scale events that span dozens of cities and involve hundreds (perhaps thousands) of volunteers, paid workers,

Arnold Donald, Chairman & Chief Executive Officer of Merisant, home of Equal® Sweetener

Equal presents America's Walk for Diabetes, a partnership of Equal and the American Diabetes Association, is a good match. When people think of diabetes, they think of sugar. So what more logical a connection than Equal, a leading sugar substitute, raising research money to find a cure for diabetes? The cause is well chosen, and the idea makes sense. (Courtesy of Merisant Company, copyright 2001. Used with permission.)

and participants. One such organization, Pallotta TeamWorks, perhaps best known for its highly successful Be the People campaigns, is credited with sending more money to AIDS and breast cancer charities between 1994 and 2000 than any known private event enterprise in U.S. history.

The involvement of corporate sponsors with socially responsible issues had fully matured by the dawn of the 21st century. Many of the issues were controversial and dramatic in the extreme yet were still mainstream enough to touch every life, home, and business in some way.

Young, dynamic companies tended to embrace "edgier" issues, commonly referred to as "hot-button issues," that often polarized segments of the market but nonetheless drew armies of loyal supporters. Larger, publicly traded, mainstream companies tended to embrace less controversial, more broadly based issues that offended or excluded the fewest numbers of people.

Finding the right cause; choosing the right partner; developing the right program; and organizing, managing, and monitoring the various components, stages, and results are not small tasks, particularly for caring companies whose main business is still that of running a business. A major commitment of time and resources is as important as the commitment of the partners to the cause itself.

Designing a Marketing Plan and the Role of Research

Just as research is important in the selection of a partner and the focus of a cause marketing program, research is an integral part of a well-crafted marketing plan. *A basic marketing plan should include a situation analysis, a statement of objectives, a strategy and tactics, a timeline, and a budget.*

It is crucial to the plan's value that the research data be collected prior to its creation and continue throughout its execution to be reliable and objective, not merely a reflection of the CEO's opinions, wishful thinking, or a marketing manager's gut feeling. Mar-

Paul Newman used his fame and influence as a film star to launch a diversified line of food products that fund a foundation and, in turn, a variety of charities. The move inspired other celebrities to develop philanthropic programs and support their chosen causes. (Photo by Karin Gottschalk Marconi)

keting is a high-stakes process that cannot put millions of corporate dollars at risk by allowing marketing directors to wet their fingers and hold them to the wind as a way of selecting a marketing plan.

Despite the fact that it may be someone's job to *say* they know, before signing off on a budget, a company must absolutely know for certain the following information:

- The market—whom are you trying to reach with your message? Break this information down to consider age, income, gender, education, geographic area, ethnicity, lifestyle, and preferences.

- How is the company, organization, or brand perceived by its customers, prospects, and other constituent groups—both by itself and compared with its competitors? What is the public's opinion of the company's industry in general? (For example, some surveys indicate that people like their own bank but have a low opinion of banks generally; respect their own lawyer but dislike lawyers in general; and this point can be made about insurance companies, automobile companies, and even business in general.) It is critical to know and understand public sentiment before committing resources to a marketing effort or cause.

- Is the company known to the media beyond its own advertising? How often has the company been the subject of media attention during the past year? Was the story positive or negative? Was it an accurate reflection of how the company sees itself? Was it consistent with other opinions of the company to appear in the media?

- Has the company been recognized or honored by its industry or its community? If so, is this widely known to the company's various constituent groups—both inside and outside the company?

- What is the company's percentage of repeat customers? What is its turnover rate, and is this higher or lower than the industry average? The answers to these questions may help to discover whether the company is perceived as a good place to work or do business with.

- Is the volume of business or level of activity cyclical or dependent on the business cycles of other industries?

- What is the company's history, if any, regarding community service, charitable participation, or philanthropic activity, both alone and relative to that of its competitors? If such participation is significant, is it widely known or credited to the company?

These are only some of the most basic points research must determine. Too often, companies dismiss such requests for research data with comments like "Everybody knows we're the best in the business" or "It's generally known that we are the leaders in the market" or, worse still, "We could not have stayed in business this long if we weren't doing something right." Corporate arrogance and inflated egos in the executive suite have helped giants that once dominated their respective markets watch market share dwindle—or plummet.

Taking the pulse of the market before and during the execution of a marketing plan can be one of the smartest investments a business can make. It is a huge and potentially expensive misstep to merely assume that a company or brand is known and loved. Research methods might include personal interviews, mail or telephone surveys, focus groups, questionnaires, or an analysis of mail, phone, and online communications from vendors, customers, shareholders, or the general public.

Know all that you can know about your market and how the public, regulators, legislators, other members of your industry, your employees, and the media perceive your company before committing to a plan.

Considerations in Picking a Partner

It is essential that a company or organization have a clear picture of itself, its strengths (or perceived strengths), and its weaknesses before choosing a cause marketing partner and undertaking a serious program. Once your own company profile has been developed, it is time to subject prospective partners to the same type of evaluation process.

Business for Social Responsibility emphasizes that "true partnerships demand honesty, integrity, respect, and mutual esteem." Being a partner in a cause marketing program does not mean a company must change its ways of doing business or pursuing its goals. On the contrary, the very principles of how a company conducts its business should be among the characteristics that make it a potentially attractive partner.

As BSR notes, "While each partner must pursue individual institutional objectives, joint objectives must be equally served. Both companies and nonprofit organizations must operate with a keen awareness of the potential risks to both partners, properly value the contributions made by each partner, and remain mindful that the rewards must be equitable." Unlike a merger, where companies agree to combine their assets and adhere to a unified set of standards and practices, cause marketing partners retain their strong individual identities and the characteristics that make them unique. That each maintains a strong identity and presence in the marketplace and pursues its own mission and objectives in its own way is part of the value each brings to the relationship.

Partnerships are often compared to marriages, with divorce statistics always in the back of one's mind. Compatibility of the partners is a key ingredient. Although it may seem that many causes would be easy to embrace as their objectives seem noble yet virtually generic—help the homeless, feed the hungry, educate those that need education, clean up the environment, fight for human rights—seemingly minor differences between potential partners about how they view such objectives could undermine a relationship.

Consider, for example, the organizational differences that typically result from dissimilar cultures: On the one hand, the business that achieves maximum efficiency through the use of such incentives as benefit plans, bonuses, and stock options and whose workforce is trained to accomplish objectives within a specific time and budget; and on the other hand, a nonprofit organization that may have some paid staff but relies largely on volunteers, whose motivation is rarely linked to compensation and who must be managed very differently.

Shirley Sagawa and Eli Segal, two experts in the management of cause-related programs, suggest that "non-profits may consider business to be 'part of the problem' and view a business partner only as a check writer; a business may believe social sector organizations foster dependency and fail to solve the problems they are created to address."

They add:

Understanding an organization's needs and assets, as well as its culture, capacity and context, are prerequisites for identifying prospective partners. These factors should guide decisions about whom to pursue and frame a "value proposition" that compellingly explains "what's in it for you." The key then is to find a partner that might respond to that value proposition; whose assets respond to your organization's needs; and whose culture, capacity, and context are compatible with yours.

The same considerations the company addressed in defining its own corporate profile should be applied to its potential partner in considering a cause marketing relationship:

- What or who is the market the cause (or nonprofit organization that represents it) seeks to reach with its message?

- How is the cause or organization perceived by the public, specifically those segments of the public the company is most concerned with reaching, influencing, and maintaining a relationship with?

- How is the cause or organization perceived by the media? Will this perception help the company's business and reputation, hurt them, or have no measurable impact whatsoever?

- Has the cause or organization been honored in any way, and, if so, was such attention positive or did it appear self-serving?

- How does this cause or organization rank or measure up to other causes or groups attempting to achieve similar objectives?

- Has the cause or organization had a consistent record, staying focused on its objectives, or has its history been inconsistent and unfocused?

- Does the cause or organization continue to attract interest, volunteers, and supporters, or does it appear that its best days are behind it?

- What about the organization's structure and management? Is its head person a paid employee or a volunteer? Does he or she have a contract with specific targets or objectives that must be met within a specific time frame? Do senior people in the organization have ties to any other organizations? (An unpaid or volunteer board chairman of a nonprofit organization may well have a salaried position at a company that sets up a conflict or issues that need to be addressed.)

The same approach a company takes in maintaining a standard for itself in terms of its commitments to *corporate social responsibility, ethics, community involvement, community economic development, the environment, accountability, human rights, concerns for the marketplace and the workplace along with its mission, vision, and values* should be considered and applied to any potential partners.

The company must be clear about what it hopes to accomplish with its cause marketing effort. If its objective is simply to improve its visibility or enhance its image, any number of highly visible programs or events will afford plenty of signage and sponsor credit. But if the aim is to alter or enhance its image with a particular constituency—perhaps the audience the company currently has, once had, or hopes to get in the future—that should narrow the field of prospective partners.

Some companies choose to partner with well-established, safe, mainstream causes or nonprofit organizations with a high degree of name recognition, high favorability ratings, a good public report card, and a scandal-free history. Many of these organizations are respected, distinguished, and do good work. Such an association will likely not hurt the company and will almost certainly add an attractive, dignified note to the corporate annual report—definitely better than nothing when rating the company on its social conscience.

But there is also the risk-reward ratio to be considered. Again, what does the company want to accomplish? A low-risk connection rates a nod of approval or a pat on the head, but by joining such a mainstream effort, the company joins others that have gone before it and, while doing good, is not likely to distinguish itself in the marketplace as unique, different, or worthy of notice. A more dramatic or distinctive partnership will likely be for higher stakes with both potential gains and potential risks to be assessed.

For example, a company that becomes a visible advocate and sponsor of an organization such as Planned Parenthood will get attention, appreciation, and very likely new customers from the constituency that supports not only this particular organization but the principles it represents. At the same time, such a relationship will also bring the company to the attention of people who strongly oppose the aims and principles of Planned Parenthood. This group will most likely not only not patronize, support, or recommend the company but will probably attempt to discourage other people from doing so. Such companies and organizations exist at both ends of the spectrum from liberal to conservative. They could hardly be called (for the most part) radical or extremist, yet they do have their constituencies that feel passionately about their causes and issues—and often take note of which companies openly contribute to or support what causes. To partner with one side opens the door to its loyal, devoted supporters while simultaneously incurring perhaps permanent disfavor among those holding the opposite point of view.

Just as a well-crafted ad campaign should appeal to a specific target market segment without excluding or alienating other market segments, a marketer must consider the potential long-term ramifications of a cause marketing effort that might eliminate the possibility of ever doing business with someone who does not share the company's interest in a particular issue or cause. As one company executive described it: "I always like to market to the target group I think is likely to hate me the least." The remark is silly but, alas, may have a certain amount of wisdom behind it.

LOGICAL CHOICES IN SELECTING A PARTNER

Nothing at all is inappropriate about a company's contributing to and supporting more than one worthwhile charity or cause. A check to United Way or participation in a blood drive does not preclude a company's having another "signature cause" with which it is strongly identified. Indeed, to create a record in which, over time, the company supports a variety of worthy causes serves to enhance the company's reputation as a good corporate citizen.

Assuming, however, that the usual constraints on a company's resources limit the selection of a cause marketing partner to just one, that one should be chosen with great care and deliberation.

Market research should have provided you with a solid sense of your company and how it is perceived as well as a profile of your target market. Before you can work this market to maximum advantage, you have to know and understand the major issues and concerns of your major constituent segments.

Some concerns, such as the desire for quality and value, can be addressed by the product or service the company provides. But the company, product, or brand image—often the pivotal factor in a consumer's choosing one company or brand over another regardless of quality and value considerations—is an emotional matter. It is an opinion or preference based on feelings. Such feelings are influenced or affected by the company's overall positioning, including its identification with issues or causes about which the consumer has strong feelings. It is the process by which cause marketing makes a difference and underscores the need for careful selection of a partner.

Evaluating Potential Partners

Identify the causes, issues, and organizations whose goals best complement those of the company. BSR recommends evaluating possible partners by reviewing these characteristics of organizations being considered:

- The organization's objectives

- The capacity of the organization to commit to, and follow through on, a cause marketing partnership

- Geographical distribution/location(s)

- The organization's history

- The composition of its board of directors

- Its leadership and financial management

- Its competition

- The relationship between the organization and its employees, volunteers, supporters, suppliers, business partners, and beneficiaries

- Its standing with local and national regulators, taxing authorities, Better Business Bureaus, and other nongovernment watchdogs

- Recent positive and negative press coverage or involvement with controversial issues

In a company of any size, it is likely that differences will exist over the selection of a cause with which to become associated. Because many people have a variety of preferences, management should create a team or committee that includes the chief financial officer and no more than three other senior executives. Once this committee is in place, compare the evaluations of each potential cause marketing partner in much the same way a management team might review the credentials and presentations of advertising agencies—comparing each organization's resources, financial stability, reputation and integrity, management structure and capabilities, accessibility and accountability, sense of priority, accomplishments, and the "chemistry" of the people who will be representing both the company and the nonprofit organization or cause once the program is under way.

Consider realistically how good or logical a fit the partner(s) would be. A high-tech company partnering with an organization whose mission is to advance education and training opportunities would seem to make good sense. A food company involved in an effort to fight hunger is a logical pairing. Companies can certainly exercise a great deal of latitude here as many issues are wide ranging and affect a broad spectrum of people. But clearly some combinations make more sense than others.

Examples of good and bad pairings. A company committed to helping find a cure for AIDS, for example, would be considered humanitarian and socially responsible by much of the public, particularly if the company's research indicates that its customer base included people in a high-risk category for the disease.

On the other hand, some matches almost seem to defy logic, such as an international clothing manufacturing and retailing operation launching a huge and expensive campaign against capital punishment. The company, primarily known for its sweaters, used various media to show dark images of prisoners on death row in many prisons. The marketplace and much of the media initially responded to this campaign with a loud "huh?"

Certainly any company in any industry has a right (perhaps, some would insist, a duty) to take a position on important social issues. In the campaign against capital punishment, however, the execution (no pun intended) of the campaign was clumsy and hard to follow, and seemed to leave the company, its brand, and its products on the sidelines, curiously disengaged from the issue or subject. People asked what the connection might be between expensive sweaters and the death penalty for convicted criminals. More important, the company failed to articulate why it chose this particular cause, which further seemed to take away from whatever effectiveness the visibility of the campaign might have had.

Had the company hoped to stimulate serious and meaningful discussion of the morality of capital punishment, it instead stimulated discussion of why a sweater company was discussing capital punishment in its marketing program. A year later, people were still talking, still asking, "What could the company have been thinking?" The question was never answered, but sweater sales continued to decline.

A cause marketing campaign, like any other good marketing campaign, must recognize that the more quickly and easily an audience can identify with the message, the more effective and successful the campaign is likely to be.

It is important that the partners in a cause marketing campaign both plan and execute the campaign together—another reason why the chemistry of the participants is important. Without a coordinated plan and a clear division of responsibility, one partner may appear to simply be attaching itself to the other's name and reputation in exchange for cash.

A prominent multinational corporation launched a lavish series of TV and print ads in which the company suggested it was responsible for a multitude of good deeds. Upon scrutiny, however, the company identified a number of nonprofit organizations that actually did the good deeds, whereas the company's role was that of contributing money to the organizations. In some cases, the company donated its products in lieu of cash.

Although the money and products may well have been substantial, the company appeared to be trying to take credit for things it did not really do. In merely writing checks, it seemed to be trying to attach its name and logo to something other entities had done— entities that existed and were known for their good work long before the company sought to identify itself with the organizations. By running several ads, each of which identified the work of a cause or organization to which the company gave money, the company, rather than identifying itself with a cause or issue about which it felt passionately committed, took a something-for-everybody approach and spread the wealth around. Finally, many of the good causes that benefited from the company's generosity by receiving donations of money or products were organizations whose purposes seemed at odds with the effects of the company's flagship products. Was this company actually counting on no member of the public ever making that connection?

In other words, a company that manufactures and sells products that the company itself concedes "are dangerous to your health" would seem to have a difficult time credibly identifying itself with organizations dedicated to helping people stay healthy.

Applying logic in the case of cause marketing partners means that the public should have no difficulty accepting a particular company and a nonprofit organization as partners. If it appears that the effort is blatantly, transparently self-serving and disingenuous, the partnership is more than just a waste of time and money but can damage the reputations of all it touches.

Determining Responsibilities

After carefully evaluating possible partners and deliberating in subsequent meetings, a company, once having determined that a certain organization would be a good fit as a cause marketing partner, must decide who will take responsibility for implementing the various components of the program. With two or more partners each seeking to benefit from the partnership, its efficient and effective management becomes a key consideration.

Appearances matter. The company has the money and wants an identification with a cause, perhaps for the noblest of purposes; the nonprofit organization has the experience, expertise, and superior knowledge of the workings and needs of the cause. Such an organization cannot afford to let a representative of a company that knows less about an issue or cause appear to be in charge. That would look like the kind of sellout that could irreparably harm the organization's reputation. Yet a company that receives no responsible role beyond providing financing risks the appearance that it knows precious little about the subject with which it would identify itself.

Assuming the partnership is a good fit and both the company and the nonprofit organization share a mutual respect, an easy solution is to create a governing board composed of members (of equal rank and status) from both camps. A staff can be put in place with newly recruited personnel as well as employees of both partners, with everyone accountable to the neutral governing board.

In situations where corporate politics and public appearances are not so highly visible—typically the case with smaller companies and local nonprofit groups—the staff is usually the more appropriate entity to manage the program, but a company representative should have more than an incidental role as liaison. To represent the company, its employees, and other stakeholders, the company's agent should have specific responsibilities, participation, and accountability.

Cause marketing has been around long enough and has evolved to a degree of sophistication that any misstep allowing one partner or the other to claim total innocence or say it was "out of the loop" should not be tolerated. Total involvement encourages total confidence from supporters and stakeholders on both sides.

The goal of the cause marketing program should be clearly spelled out in writing. The division of responsibilities should be written as should summaries of each meeting. This is often considered a "cover-your-rear-end" procedure, but people don't always recall what was said or agreed—or they remember such things differently. A written mission statement, objectives, and assignment roster literally put everyone on the same page, minimizing confusion and misunderstanding.

The importance of reliable, current research at most stages of the program cannot be emphasized strongly enough. To undertake a cause marketing effort (or any marketing effort for that matter) without having clearly determined what a company's constituents and the general public think of the company is like heading out to sea without navigational tools.

How a cause marketing partner is perceived and how the two partners appear to complement one another is critical information. Unless a company has a clear feeling for these questions and their answers, the cause marketing plan is being constructed on very shaky ground. Listening to the voice of the market is the shortest route to cost-effective planning and partnering.

S U M M A R Y

- Research is an essential part of any marketing plan, especially a cause marketing plan.

- Know all you can know about how both the company and the nonprofit organization are perceived by the public, regulators, members of your industry, investors, the media, and other stakeholders before committing to a plan.

- Each partner in a cause marketing effort must pursue individual institutional objectives, but joint objectives must be equally served.

- In choosing a cause marketing partner, a company must look for an organization that understands its needs and whose culture, capabilities, and context are compatible with its own.

- A well-crafted campaign should appeal to a specific target without excluding or alienating the rest of the market.

- The choice of a cause marketing partner should be logical. If the public or stakeholders have to be convinced the partnership was a good idea, it probably wasn't a good idea.

- Create a list of evaluation standards for the company's cause marketing effort.

- Form a committee or task force to apply evaluation standards to prospective organizations.

- Apply the standards and consider possible causes as you would review presentations from prospective ad agencies.

- Consider a partner based on its resources, financial stability, integrity, capabilities, accessibility, accountability, and "chemistry" with members of the other side's team.

  IDF ~ Idyll
- Partners in a cause marketing campaign should plan and execute the campaign together, with a clear division of responsibility.

- Spell out plans and assignments in writing to keep the program on track, noting the mission statement, objectives, and division of responsibility.

3

The Company, the Cause, the Community, and the World

Logically, a global company that sees its market as the world would likely expect its association with a cause to be worldwide in scope and significance. Or would it? Ronald McDonald House was the international fast-food giant's first important charitable venture, a haven for families wanting to be near children receiving major medical treatment in local hospitals.

A relatively small local company might seem ridiculous if it were to align itself with a cause-related program that sought to help people on the other side of the globe, where its local customers didn't see the faraway needy families but did see major concerns much closer to home. Right? Maybe not.

Network TV news broadcasts and national magazines routinely report on famine, flood, earthquake, and wars in which children are left homeless and seemingly without hope unless someone reaches into both heart and wallet to help in some meaningful way. Cause marketing is specifically about helping people in a meaningful way that will in turn reflect back favorably on the doer of the good work. CARE, UNICEF, the International Red Cross, and countless others appeal to companies and individuals without concern for borders, viewing their constituents as the community of the world.

And yet few communities can claim not to have needs they perceive to be just as important as the tragedies occurring a world away.

Hunger, homelessness, illiteracy, and life-threatening diseases are not exclusively the concerns of impoverished third-world nations. The company must determine where its support will do the most good for the greatest number of people and, at the same time, be recognized for its effects by people whose goodwill it needs to remain in business.

Sometimes a company's resources are very limited, and it is best advised to contribute to a national organization (or at least the local chapter of a national organization) in which its contributions can be combined with those of other companies to do more good. Can a small New England ice cream company really expect to save the rain forests? If it contributes a portion of the money received from each of its products sold to an organization set up to do just that—yes, it can make a difference. At the same time, a local company that helps to fund a local homeless shelter or a safe haven for abused women and children is addressing a problem on a local level that society understands is part of a larger cultural issue.

From the lists of worthy causes, the company must recognize that if it indeed has only limited resources, it must choose a cause that seems (1) appropriate to its business and its region, (2) of concern to its own stakeholders, and (3) compatible with its corporate position and mission.

Having identified a prospective partner for a cause marketing program, a number of issues must be addressed before the program can get underway. Some issues are mechanical and operational, such as who will do what and how; some are legal, as who has ownership of the material and responsibility for payments. In addition, there is the scope of the program—how far and wide the effort will reach.

Partnership agreements can be complicated, even if they apply only to a single project of limited duration. Regulations, requirements, and laws can differ from city to city and state to state. And if the Internet will be a vehicle employed for information or promotion, is the "universe without borders" a universe of opportunities or a potential minefield?

The late Thomas P. "Tip" O'Neill, former Massachusetts congressman and Speaker of the U.S. House of Representatives, is credited with making famous the phrase *All politics is local.* It can be assumed he meant that no matter how exalted the office— whether a seat in Congress, the presidency, or secretary-general of the UN—it is wise to remember that each individual voter is first concerned with how the prospective office holder's candidacy and subsequent performance will benefit him or her. The smart candidate, while being mindful of the big picture, will always appreciate the importance of self-interests among constituents and build a base of support one voter at a time until a majority is achieved. The same can be said of marketing.

The most powerful companies, organizations, and brands with connections, customers, investors, and supporters around the world gain and lose support and market share one customer, purchase, or contributor at a time.

In cause marketing, a company and its prospective nonprofit organization partner must determine the activities on which it will focus. Will the cause be local—that is, centered on a particular city or community—or will it be national or global? With Speaker O'Neill's words of wisdom still echoing, the company's management must understand the value of, and need for, effectively communicating the company's (and the cause's) message to its full contingent of stakeholders and constituents as personal, no matter how important the issue may be in its reach.

People are aware of who are and who are not good neighbors. It is admirable in business to aim for the sky, but it takes good business sense and good marketing to know what is happening on the corner and, perhaps most important, inside the company.

STARTING FROM THE INSIDE

Causes chosen for consideration by companies are almost by definition emotional issues, and emotions are extremely personal. It is reasonable to expect that not everyone in the company will agree with management's choice of a cause and may very well want to let their lack of enthusiasm be known. Such an action could be destructive if it is not addressed early, and it can severely undermine or even sabotage the program.

Management (at all levels) and employee support for the cause marketing decision is critical to its potential success. Like the company's advertising, public relations, and overall marketing plan, cause marketing cannot achieve its maximum potential if senior staff, who influence and manage others throughout the organization, don't accept its value to the company and fully commit to its objectives.

Files of fact and folklore contain stories of CEOs who said they never understood their ads but were glad when they worked. Or who claimed they didn't believe in advertising. No amount of agency research data would convince them. But cause marketing is unique in that *belief* is a key ingredient in the public's response to the program. If the company has not succeeded in convincing its own people of the good of the cause, it will not likely convince those outside the company.

Management can inspire and motivate staff participation; promote the program to decision makers and personnel in all departments, facilities, locations, and business units; and publicize the value of the program to all stakeholders, both internally and externally, as well as to existing supporters of the cause the company wants to know. It may well be a formidable task—perhaps even a challenge—but it is essential to the effort's succeeding.

BSR's cause-related marketing partnership guidelines stress that the cause marketing plan must be clear to all who are involved. A productive, well-coordinated program cannot succeed if each partner's internal machinery is not operating properly. Before the plan can be effectively implemented, much less communicated, what that plan encompasses must be clear.

Define the Program

To be successful, a cause marketing effort must begin with a good idea that has been thoroughly researched before being implemented. Many of the most successful campaigns have been constructed around effectively defined messages that clearly define benefits. Such a well-defined program should consider:

- The creative idea
- The balance between the benefits to the cause as well as to the business
- The range of the products and services involved
- A timeline
- The division of labor
- Whether the goals of the program are realistic and achievable in the current market climate, if at all
- The communications messages and strategy
- The mechanism for evaluating the program
- Options for expanding and concluding the program

Assess the Risks

As in any type of business relationship that affords benefits, a cause marketing program will likely also have potential risks to both partners. It is important to carefully and thoughtfully review the proposed program for potential risks to all parties, including worst-case scenarios. Consider and evaluate what BSR regards as the *five key risk areas:*

1. Reputation

2. Internal policies and practices

3. Legal matters

4. Resource allocation

5. Logistics

Define the Value of the Opportunity

Certainly from every perspective, but most important as a matter of bringing all members of the company staff and management on board, establishing a clear appreciation for the program (if not for the cause itself) is important to evaluate its success. The program should have identifiable *value elements,* which may include the following:

- Overall benefits to the business

- Overall benefits to the community

- Increased awareness

- Enhanced reputation

- A significant impact on employee recruitment and retention

- Product or service differentiation

- A powerful public relations message

It is important that key players understand and consider anything and everything that will add to the value of the cause marketing program when they are negotiating and finalizing the terms of the agreement between the partners, the formulation of the plan, and how the entire program will be communicated to employees and other stakeholders. Clearly the attention drawn to the cause marketing program will likely raise the profiles of both the company and the nonprofit organization, perhaps enabling either or both partners to attract additional resources and supporters.

BSR points out that in finalizing an agreement between the partners, private companies and nonprofit organizations have independent obligations to comply with *all applicable laws.*

Within the United States, each state and many local governments have fundraising and sponsorship registration requirements. Several states require companies and nonprofit organizations working as partners in any type of venture to have a written contract. Requirements may vary from state to state and must be researched and addressed before an agreement can become final. In essence, one agreement can be in effect for a cause marketing effort in one particular community, but a wholly separate agreement may be required if the program were to be expanded to a three-state or five-state area where requirements could be significantly different in each state, particularly with regard to registration or other applicable laws.

Should the partners choose to broaden the program to include other *countries,* again all applicable laws must be researched and addressed. It is reasonable to expect different countries to have different laws and requirements for cause-related programs, particularly those involving commercially funded nonprofit organizations.

All legal and financial issues, as well as the issue of who will assume responsibility for which aspects and components of the program, should be clearly spelled out in the agreement between the partners. Such matters as what is to be accomplished, whether the program will continue open-ended or be limited to a particular season or event, ownership of the rights to the program for future or residual use, and the management of trademarks and graphics are relatively simple to address. Yet they illustrate how much can go wrong if the simple issues are not clearly defined.

A cause marketing program is more than a company and a nonprofit organization announcing their good intentions, raising money for a good cause, and winning rave notices in the media. It is first a business agreement with all the legal reporting and filing requirements, along with management and scrutiny, that characterizes any other business arrangement.

The partners should identify the following items in writing:

- The primary purpose of the partnership

- The names of all parties bound by the agreement, including suppliers, agencies, and any third parties or subcontractors

- The roles and responsibilities of everyone involved at each stage

- The duration of the agreement

- Scheduled and unscheduled activities and timeline

- Status and ownership of material, including intellectual property rights

- The agreed use and ownership of logos, names, graphics, slogans, publications, photographs, and other such materials

- The process for approving copy, photos, logos, themes, and the like

- An organization chart and/or protocol for project reporting

- Details regarding arrangements for the funding and management of resources

- Policy and schedule regarding payments

- Details of an evaluation plan and its implementation

- Provisions relating to the extension or termination of the agreement, including an exit strategy

- The process enabling expansion into other markets

The agreement might also have a provision covering *minimum guarantees*. For example, the partners may agree to a minimum guarantee for the funding and delivery of services. Although each partnership and cause marketing program should be unique, there should be certain considerations that are fairly common to most partnerships.

A corporate partner will usually agree to cover costs incurred by the nonprofit partner within predetermined limits. It is also important to establish in the agreement how such matters as budget overruns will be handled, as well as the allocation of funds and management responsibility should the program exceed its goals or expectations.

ISSUES OF EXCLUSIVITY: YOU AND WHO ELSE?

It is extremely important for partners in the agreement to be clear about matters of *exclusivity* in both the development stage and throughout the duration of the program. A partnership that involves a company and a nonprofit organization must be clear whether the same nonprofit organization may or will enter into partnerships with other companies and, if so, under what circumstances and with what limitations. Similarly, is the company free and willing to form partnerships with other nonprofits and, if so, which organization will be designated as having priority in the company's marketing plans and materials?

Considerations that might appropriately be addressed include:

- Time limitations and restrictions, if any

- The geographic areas in which any or all partnerships may or may not be created

- Limitations or restrictions, if any, regarding particular product categories, cause sectors, or competitive industries

- The types of activities involved

This is not as clear-cut an area as it once was now that businesses are so well aware of the concept of "conflict of interest." It would hardly seem appropriate nor make any marketing sense for the same spokesperson to be representing two products in the same category, so how would it make sense to have the same cause-related program underwritten by two competing companies or brands?

The short version is that it would *not* make sense—that the most effective partnerships involve one company and one nonprofit organization linking their names in the public consciousness. The new reality is that the old rules no longer apply and such nonexclusive relationships are increasingly more common, largely related to the importance and visibility of the issue or cause on the public landscape.

Ben & Jerry's ice cream, for example, has long been identified with efforts to save the rain forests and promote environmental issues. For the company to announce that it would now also help fund literacy programs would be totally consistent with its corporate image and might greatly please the company's core constituency, a group that considers the company to have a highly focused sense of responsibility. However, the announcement would most likely not please environmentalist organizations that, while socially responsible, look to the company for financial support, which could possibly be diluted by the company's expanding its cause marketing activity.

And would the company's customers view such a move as the company's showing it had an even greater desire to do well by doing good, or would it imply a diminished commitment to causes with which it had been identified more closely in the past? A specific provision in the agreement would at least have made the issue clear to the partners, each of whom would then know what it might reasonably expect from the other.

Although exclusive partnerships are the most common, notable exceptions can be found. The annual Muscular Dystrophy telethon receives more money on a single day than had been collected throughout the year by various retailers, many of whom were competitors doing business not only in the same market but in the same shopping center as well.

A large-scale event to raise money for AIDS research or a concert to benefit the families of victims of a disaster routinely attracts multiple sponsors, sometimes from the same industry or sometimes well known for their identification with other causes. In such cases, a company may be willing, or even eager, to see its name listed among names of competitors rather than appear to its public as having a lesser degree of concern than its competitors for the issue or cause.

Again, the marketing value of participating or not participating can be considered as a separate issue, but the partnership agreement between the company and the nonprofit can eliminate any misunderstanding or bad feeling before such matters become issues.

MANAGING THE PROGRAM

Just as an agreement is critical, so too is the decision of who will be responsible for overseeing its implementation. The strongest partnerships and the best ideas can be put at risk without the right management.

BSR advises that at the project management level, the following issues should be addressed:

- The scope of the work and timeliness of the program

- Primary contacts

- Budgets

- Decision-making process

- Designation of responsibilities for all aspects of the process

- Communication procedures

- Success criteria and measurement process

Depending on the size and scope of the cause marketing program, some partnerships designate a staff person or team, others hire a manager, and still others vest management responsibility in the hands of outside professionals, firms that specialize in managing just such programs. As interest in cause marketing continues to grow, so do the number of firms and companies claiming to have expertise in the area. It is important, however, to understand the difference between an event manager and a program manager. A company that can manage a setup crew, drivers, caterers, musicians, service personnel, sound system, and traffic flow is not necessarily qualified to manage media, volunteers, travel arrangements, a diverse staff with diverse responsibilities, fundraising, accounting, and legal needs.

Pallotta TeamWorks, a Los Angeles–based company with an impressive track record refereed to earlier, refuses to be limited to describing itself as a fundraising company or an event manager, though it managed some 27 major fundraising events in 2001 alone. The firm works with organizations to provide coaching, training, fundraising techniques and pretested forms, support staff, and transportation for events.

This type of consulting/training/support can be an efficient and useful resource for a manager, but hiring such a firm is not a substitute for a manager who is an integral part of the program's day-to-day activities and content. Remembering the important legal and regulatory filing responsibilities common to cause marketing programs and partnerships, as well as the need to effectively manage and coordinate internal and external communications, it is essential that management of the program be vested in a person with managerial skills, experience, and an ability to access and oversee needed outside resources.

THE ART OF COMMUNICATION

A company choosing a good cause with which to identify itself and do good work and then forming a partnership with a nonprofit organization that can work with the company to share its vision and achieve its goals is a highly significant development in a company of any size. The announcement and subsequent communications should reflect the importance of this decision and action. It is not simply a public relations moment to be described in a press release; it is a marketing event of major proportions and may be incorporated and reflected in packaging, pricing, and sales of the company's products and services.

Announcing the Program and Partnership

Treat the announcement of the program and the partnership as the important event that it is. Just as most people like to share news first with the people closest to them, the first announcement of the cause marketing partnership should be an internal one to staff and stakeholders of the company. Consider taking these 12 steps:

Step 1: A letter to company shareholders or investors should announce the company's pride and excitement about the partnership and briefly note ways in which the company will likely benefit.

Step 2: If possible, call a meeting of all employees or, at least, most departments. Or managers of each department or branch location should call meetings of their people (simultaneously) to announce the partnership and enthusiastically explain how the company will benefit.

Step 3: The public announcement should either briefly follow, or occur simultaneously with, the internal announcement. *Make sure the company's employees and investors don't first learn of the partnership in a newspaper account.* Company employees are likely to be asked about the partnership by anyone from their next door neighbors to news reporters, and they should be able to say they are aware of the cause-related program, feel as if they are a part of it, and endorse it.

Step 4: If a meeting or series of meetings within the company is not possible, at a minimum send each employee a memo, on paper or by e-mail, before or at the same time as the public announcement is being made. Before the rest of the world knows, the memo is a courtesy. Learning about the program after the public announcement may be viewed by some employees as a slight on the part of management, but it is also a lost opportunity to generate enthusiastic support and good word of mouth.

Step 5: Designate an *employee delegate* to the cause marketing program who can answer questions and disseminate information and literature, buttons, bumper stickers, T-shirts, lapel pins, stickers, or similar materials.

Step 6: Initiate a newsletter that provides employees with information about the cause and keeps enthusiasm high.

Step 7: For a formal announcement, many companies instinctively think of having a press conference. In the modern age of communication, unless the company is on a level with the Pentagon, Microsoft, or Disney, a press conference is inappropriate. Most reporters will not attend or will only confirm their attendance at the last minute, asking instead to receive material relating to the announcement—a request the company cannot ignore without acting against its own interests.

Better than a press conference in most instances is the *video news release*, which offers more control and greater presentation flexibility and can be sent electronically or by messenger to key media with great efficiency. Print media should still receive hard copy press releases with background information on both partners, photos, and any relevant additional material.

Representatives of both the company and the nonprofit organization should be available by phone during a designated period for questions and to provide additional quotes.

Step 8: Although the company and the nonprofit organization should make a joint announcement, a single spokesperson should be designated as the contact who will answer questions, arrange interviews, and provide needed information, materials, and access.

Step 9: Consider *the message*—its content, tone, and style. Does it correctly convey what you want the public to know and feel about the company, the nonprofit organization, and the cause?

Step 10: BSR research indicates that all methods of communication are seen as appropriate by consumers provided that the message is balanced and the mutual benefits clear.

Step 11: Identify your audience and determine what messages you want to communicate to them, how often, and in what manner.

Step 12: Anticipate questions and provide answers in advance.

In a time of increasing cynicism, a company that commits itself to supporting a good cause has an opportunity to stand out and win support and goodwill that ultimately produces benefits to the company. It is a simple matter of *doing well by doing good.* But by drawing attention in a time of cynicism, it is highly likely that the company's motives as well as its methods will be closely scrutinized. For this reason (as well as because it is the ethical thing to do), the company must be sure it can withstand such scrutiny and that its message is credible and sincere.

As much as it is possible, provide specifics. Tell what portion or percentage of revenue derived from sales of the company's products or services will be used to benefit the cause or issue. Be as specific as possible in stating the company's commitment to the cause in dollars over an announced period. Indicate if the company's relationship with the nonprofit is open-ended, for a season only, for the duration of the program, or linked to a one-time-only event or date as well as what guarantees, if any, have been made and can be discussed.

It is usually to the partnership's best advantage to be honest, but some judgment is necessary as to how such honesty should be represented. For example, Sears was sponsoring a concert to raise money to benefit homeless Americans. A reporter was covering the concert when he came upon a Sears executive who, seeing a chance for some publicity, told the reporter that he was certain the concert "would provide a compelling reason for people to shop at Sears."

Groan. The quotation made the pages of a high-circulation weekly business magazine. It implied that the commitment to help the homeless was hardly the reason the store had opened its heart and its checkbook. The same point could have been made by saying "We're here to reinforce in people's minds that Sears cares about people and wants to help." Such a statement would have actually provided a "compelling reason for people to shop at Sears."

UNDERSTANDING BENEFITS

Shirley Sagawa and Eli Segal make the point that essentially both the socially responsible company and the socially active nonprofit organization can profit in ways beyond the obvious potential for public relations benefits and community goodwill. Quoting from *Reinventing Government* by David Osborne and Ted Gaebler, they note that nonprofits can follow the example of successful businesses and learn to be:

- *Competitive,* creating incentives for higher performance

- *Customer driven,* meeting needs of clients

- *Results oriented,* focusing on outcomes, not input

- *Enterprising,* generating revenues, not just spending

- *Market oriented,* leveraging change rather than controlling it

To illustrate the other side of the partnership's benefits, Sagawa and Segal quote management guru Peter Drucker that business can learn from the social sector how to be:

- *Mission driven,* making decisions based on mission rather than on money

- *Board led,* holding the CEO accountable to the board

- *Attractive employers,* motivating staff (and volunteers) to be more productive and committed

Entering into a cause marketing partnership should be much more than exploiting the value in the names and reputations of the partners. It affords opportunities to both sides at the same time it is doing good to benefit others. Joint planning sessions, for example, not only allow each side to be clear about goals and strategies but to take advantage of each other's creative strengths and problem-solving abilities. Two entities that come together and commit to a shared vision and goals should bring the best of their respective talents to the table and should then both be bright enough to take away what ideas can be put to good use.

EVALUATING THE PROGRAM

Reviewing, measuring, and evaluating the effectiveness of the partnership is a clearly understood marketing discipline, a requirement of good business management that can provide valuable information to both the company and its partner organization. BSR advises its members to evaluate the accomplishments of the initiative against its original goals and expectations throughout the duration of the program and at its conclusion. This evaluation should include a summary of the tangible benefits that resulted and the actual use of human, financial, and other resources accessed for the program.

Under most circumstances, marketers realize the importance of being willing to change in response to changes in the market. In a cause-related effort, both sides should be flexible about changing the partnership structure or process at any point in the relationship, based on experiences in working with the organization and on whether the relationship is meeting its expectations. Weigh the benefits of a long-term partnership with one organization against those that might be gained by pursuing new partnership arrangements and other programs.

Record both qualitative and anecdotal data while the program is in effect; in addition, based on agreed-upon performance indicators, attempt to measure:

- The impact on the issue or cause

- Funds raised

- Effect on sales, volume and/or traffic

- Attitude and usage tracking studies focusing on the development of stakeholder opinions regarding the organization, products, projects, brands, or services

- Media coverage

- Testimonial letters

- Effect on reputation, image, and/or awareness of both partners

- Customer satisfaction

- Employee satisfaction

- Other stakeholder satisfaction

Review the results of this evaluation to determine if or how the program has succeeded.

BSR considers an evaluation of the results relating to the partnership equal to, if not more important than, the results of a single program. Consider the value the association between the company and the nonprofit organization has brought to both entities—their employees, reputations, stakeholders, and bottom lines. When partnerships work, they can minimize the use of resources, while maximizing the positive impact on both the company and the cause.

When a partnership is *not* working, be realistic and make changes. A great deal of financial and other resources are wasted when managers refuse to cut their losses and acknowledge, as the old Indian chief said in *Little Big Man* of the failed rain dance, "Sometimes the magic works . . . and sometimes it doesn't."

VOLUNTEERS

A good cause can ignite passions, stir emotions, and, at the least, elicit interest from people who may feel strongly about the value of the cause and volunteer to help. These volunteers are important for several reasons:

- Obvious enormous cost savings occur when people offer to work long hours for no pay.

- Volunteers often bring a level of commitment and dedication to the cause that paid staffers sometimes lack.

- Volunteers often provide a rich pool of talent that the cause could not afford to enlist at any price. This might include older people—perhaps retired with brilliant CEO-level experience and skill for the price of a cup of coffee—as well as young people eager to both network and make good on commitments to community service. Both young and old volunteers bring a mix of experience, energy, talent, creativity, and fresh ideas.

- Volunteers have the ability by their example to attract and recruit other volunteers.

- The presence of volunteers sends a message to constituents that people care enough about the cause to give their time and energy for no financial gain; and this dedication is a strong point in favor of the cause.

It is essential that volunteers, whether relatively few or an army spread across a wide region, be recognized and appreciated. How the partners treat their volunteers can be critical to recruiting, productivity, and the overall image of the effort. Awards and recognition must take the place of financial compensation. Taking volunteers for granted or treating them as if they are less important or less valuable than paid staff is not only bad management but highly dangerous to the reputation of the program and the partners.

BOTH NEAR AND FAR: DECIDING THE EXTENT
OF THE PROGRAM'S AREA

If the cause marketing program is exclusively local, such as support of a local shelter, a school or public area, or a local environmental effort, make certain the community knows about it. Use the local media, signage, and all forms of communication (employee newsletters and bulletin boards, and contact with local community groups and merchants who have their own communication vehicles) to praise volunteers and publicize the mission, its successes, and the role of the partners.

If the company and the cause are being represented on a broader scale, such as citywide or statewide, nationally or internationally, make certain that people are designated to handle both local and overall communications. Obviously, the local person will promote local successes and activities, noting ways in which the community will benefit from the program.

The comprehensive communications person should publicize overall success and activities but should secondarily emphasize the number of regions or communities involved in the effort, the number of volunteers, and the total number of people who benefit from the program. Such publicity can have a very positive and synergistic effect on both the overall marketplace and participating individuals. For example, a small group of volunteers and staff in a given area may have only modest success commensurate with their resources. But by publicizing the overall success of a program that is benefiting a number of participating communities, such as [single out the community by name], which is receiving [list one or more benefits], the small group's success could be ensured. Note how [that community] can share in the reflected glow from the program's success, even if local participation is not quite as strong as it is in other communities.

Presenting an illusion of success without being dishonest or misrepresenting facts can trigger interest and attention to specific communities, and such interest can translate into new support, contributions, and/or volunteers.

THE INTERNET—A COMMUNITY WITHOUT BORDERS

With years of results to study, word of mouth continues to be the least expensive and most effective form of promotion for products, issues, and messages. It carries the benefit of a real or implied endorsement, often from a known source who attaches his or her credibility to the information. News of the company's partnership with a nonprofit organization on behalf of a cause in a company newsletter or in local media is also effective, costs little, and can be easily accomplished.

Since the 1990s, the Internet has added a new dimension to positioning, publicizing, promoting, and marketing. Presenting and receiving information through people's personal computers affords the ability to connect vast numbers of people in the most personal way 24 hours a day with minimal intrusion—unlike, for example, telemarketing, which is often effective but costly and highly intrusive.

The Internet was once touted as the ultimate means by which people would communicate, learn, buy, and sell in addition to managing their personal and business lives. After all the hype subsided (and after thousands of overvalued technology companies failed to deliver on their promise), a public backlash led to a lessening of confidence in the Internet. Ultimately, the maturing of the Internet environment has been producing a mechanism that, like print, radio, television, outdoor signs, and mail, serves as a superb means of communication that can be as public or private and as timely as its participants desire.

Marketers must understand the demographics and psychographics of both frequent and occasional Internet audiences, as well as their actual and potential size and interest levels. Reliable research data remain sketchy, and no medium has shown as much wishful thinking as fast or on so large and dangerous a scale.

Web sites, whether for business, institutions, or causes, are basically electronic catalogs, billboards, and newsletters; e-mails can be considered, like traditional mailings, desirable and welcome personal communications, or they can be dismissed as junk mail. Marketers have been known to forget these points, having gotten caught up in "tech fever" and become so excited with the colorful and interactive video game aspects of some Web sites and e-messages that they lose sight of the fact that marketing is still a verb—an active process that requires an action mechanism.

People must be brought to Web sites—attracted, lured, seduced, even hooked. Millions of dollars have been wasted on the design and construction of sites under a "field-of-dreams" scenario (where the answer to all the really difficult questions is "If you build it, they will come"). Tens of thousands of Web sites became dazzling billboards on corners no one passed. Just as any ad, brochure, or catalog—no matter how wonderful it looks, feels, or reads—is useless if no one sees it, a Web site unaccompanied by a marketing plan with a strategy for delivering visitors is as useless as an unopened copy of the Yellow Pages, only a good deal more expensive.

A cause marketing program on the Internet requires the same type of strategic plan. A good company, a good cause, and a well-constructed message is pointless if people can't find it. Even worse is if people find the site but become impatient or develop negative feelings about its owner because they have to wait for dazzling graphics or clever animation to fill the screen. Without question, designers can create wonderful graphics for the Web, but marketers need images and messages that catch and hold the attention of people who did not come to wait.

A significant aspect of marketing is the importance of delivering the message and the product quickly and directly to the market-place. The rush to establish an Internet presence in the late 1990s ignored many principles about quickness and directness and per-mitted talented designers and technology specialists to build costly sites and programs that were neither easy to navigate nor particu-larly efficient. Few companies or products are so hot that the pub-lic will patiently search for them or painstakingly indulge the company's fancy, clicking through icons and pages, searching and asking to be sold.

Despite the fact that a cause marketing program may be socially responsible, meaningful, and of enormous benefit to many, the program is nonetheless a *marketing* program and, as such, must bring the message to the public in the easiest and most direct way on the public's terms, not the marketer's.

It is often said that on the Internet, with its borderless universe, someone in Europe or South America can access a site in New York City as easily and quickly as can someone in New York City. When everything works as it should, that statement is correct. However, the person in Europe or South America must (1) know the site exists, (2) know how to access the site, and (3) want to access the site. To address these three points is what makes the effort a mar-keting effort, dependent on principles that involve packaging, pric-ing, positioning, and promotion.

Internet communication can be extremely cost effective or it can be devastatingly expensive. Technical problems can be costly to correct and highly frustrating to all who depend on the system for presenting and promoting information. The term *the system is down* has come to represent potentially nightmarish situations that tele-phone companies and television networks never dreamed of.

Having delivered that dark report, it is also true that the Internet and the World Wide Web represent a potential marketplace and mechanism for reaching unprecedented numbers of people with more specialized and customized information faster and, in some cases, far less expensively than anything previously known to marketers, manufacturers, service providers, buyers, sellers, and educators. What must be understood is *how* to use the Internet in ways that will appeal to and serve the desired target market.

There are literally tens of millions of Web sites, thousands of search engines tapping into hundreds of millions of references and entries, and a universe of service providers that expands and contracts dramatically each season, causing many companies and sites no end of grief as they scramble to stay up and running.

A very effective TV commercial showed the management team of an obviously young company gathered around a computer screen to witness the launch of its new Web site, nervously hoping it would work and people would respond. A burst of applause was heard as it worked beautifully. The applause turned to cheers as the first few incoming orders turned to hundreds of orders. The cheers grew louder as the orders mounted into the thousands, and then the reactions turned quieter, followed seemingly by terror as numbers grew to tens of thousands and kept on going. How would the young organization even be able to acknowledge, much less fill, so many orders? And what of the reliability of the system to handle so much information? And the often overlooked (and unbudgeted) consideration that businesses are typically charged a fee for the number of hits to their Web sites—fees which can mount up quickly and often are not able to be passed along as an expense buried in the "handling" charges?

A well-planned cause marketing program should indeed have its own Web site—with links to the Web sites of participating sponsor companies, partnering nonprofit organizations, and other related parties—because it is expected and assumed in the 21st century that any worthwhile program will have such a site.

However, as is often the case with some marketing programs, the Web site should not be either the centerpiece or the sole marketing and information vehicle employed. The public, contributors, volunteers, and supporters still largely expect and want printed materials, toll-free phone numbers, and a live person available to answer questions, solve problems, and promote enthusiasm for the program. Technology has been used unsuccessfully in marketing as a cost-cutting measure for replacing press kits, brochures, bumper stickers, buttons, flags, media alerts, promotional items, and public relations specialists.

Answering media questions and requests with the phrase "just go to our Web site—it's all listed there" has become a sure method of *not* winning media coverage and support. Likewise, directing volunteers and contributors or, worse, prospective volunteers and contributors to look up information that should be available in any format that will help generate a positive response is not good marketing or management.

A Web site and a coordinated, well-timed series of e-mails should be part of the program's information system but should not be the entire system.

Online auctions, utilizing a computer program similar to that of the popular and successful eBay Web site, have become excellent tools for fundraising and for promoting a cause marketing effort. Annual or frequently scheduled live auctions, often conducted as part of a formal dinner event or an evening of entertainment, have long been recognized as effective devices to promote goodwill; solicit donations of auction items from local, national, or international businesses that might otherwise not contribute to the cause; recognize volunteers; and use publicity for the auction as a way of publicizing the cause.

Through the online auction, marketers have a vehicle that expands the event and invites the participation of people around the world—people who might otherwise not bid simply because of their inability to attend. Even though the online component can expand the event geographically and extend its bidding period beyond the normal couple of hours a live event uses, the most effective system is to present an online auction that leads up to and culminates in the actual live event. This approach offers a best-of-all-worlds scenario in which non-computer-oriented supporters can participate. As popular as auctions are, the traditional auction system typically limits participation to attendees and their designated agents.

Popular online auctions attract potential worldwide participants who learn of the event and the site but exclude those who don't have access or an inclination to participate in computer-only events. An important element of successful marketing is to avoid excluding any potential market segment. By combining the online auction with the live event and publicizing both, a potentially modest local event can take on global proportions and significance.

Similarly, a live concert staged to raise money and generate awareness and support for an issue or cause can use a Web site with a program like an online auction to collect funds much as a telethon does and thereby build a database faster and more efficiently than any telephone or surface mail system could possibly match. Such a concert could also be broadcast over the Internet to an audience geographically unable to attend the event in person. Again, the entire project must be supported by a marketing plan and campaign that includes appropriate pricing, positioning, and promotion.

Demographic studies have shown the Internet to be far less traveled by older segments of the market than by younger people. In a cause marketing program, as in any other well-planned marketing program, the first rule is *know your audience*. Understand that a cause, event, issue, auction, concert, or presentation most likely to appeal to older audiences won't find its greatest response in an Internet-only format. However, to broaden the appeal of the presentation and widen the presentation itself, having it emanate from multiple locations and connect with its participants in a way that may have been cost prohibitive using television—and having it publicized well—an Internet component will greatly increase its prospects for success both inside and well beyond the borders of the local community.

How does one determine if local or wider interest in a cause exists? There is no single or simple answer, although sometimes it's simply common sense, and other times the answer is dictated by extraordinary circumstances. Raising funds to support a neighborhood halfway house or shelter will likely not attract interest outside of the neighborhood itself, unless the neighborhood partnership is one regional part of a larger cooperative group organized to address the issues of the need for halfway houses across the country. An area that is hard hit by fire, an earthquake, a hurricane, or other natural disaster—or the target of an attack by outside forces that creates devastation far beyond what might occur in the normal course of events—will likely receive wide attention and a willingness to help from caring individuals, businesses, and corporations well outside of the community.

The current cause marketing response to such situations is a function of the participating partnerships, the positioning of the issue or cause, and the manner in which such an effort is managed. Past examples have been everything from the purchase and delivery of food and medical supplies underwritten by socially responsible businesses to sales of books, shirts, and compact discs whose proceeds go to relief organizations.

In the final analysis, *all marketing is local.*

THE IMPORTANCE OF STAYING FOCUSED

In some situations, even good intentions can lead to marketing overload. Marketers have to stay focused and remain clear about what they are marketing. At the center of the program should be the subject—the company, product, organization or brand—with the cause positioned as the supporting or secondary subject, as in *buy the product and help the cause.*

Or the focus may be on the cause with the product positioned as the supporting or secondary subject, as in *help the cause each time you buy the product.*

Too often, audiences can be easily confused by a clutter of messages. As a general rule, too many logos in an ad dilute its impact and cloud its purpose. Keeping the presentation simple can actually make it more powerful. This is even truer in the overall marketing campaign. No matter how gracious and well intentioned, too many credits—acknowledgments thanking all the individuals and companies that make an event, campaign, or program successful—slow down momentum. Lists of the "many wonderful and generous people who made all this possible" are of real interest only to the wonderful and generous people themselves. There are rare exceptions to this, such as four or five companies that each contribute more than $1 million to underwrite the cost of a major event.

One particular American Express campaign had a noble, extremely important, and powerful cause as its beneficiary, but its execution was clumsy, and the campaign suffered in part from marketing overload, an abundance of names and logos. The Charge Against Hunger program, which donated a specific amount of money to help feed hungry people during the holiday season every time someone used an American Express card to make a purchase, carried five separate trademarked logos of the company's various credit cards in a heavily run series of ads. A program that stresses the kindness of the sponsors to the extent that the kindness is better remembered than the cause itself has its priorities misplaced. If the cause is so prominently positioned as to make the program a success, the sponsor will be rewarded for its generosity without having to upstage the subject itself.

The very fact of social responsibility implies a certain degree of humility or understatement that helps a company *do well by doing good.*

S U M M A R Y

- A company with limited resources may want to consider contributing to a large national cause where its contributions can be combined with those of others to do greater good.

- It is important to be clear in a partnership about who will do what and how. Satisfy ownership issues, regulatory requirements, and budget matters in written agreements.

- All marketing is local. Companies, organizations, and brands with supporters around the world must satisfy the needs and concerns of customers and constituents one at a time.

- Support for the cause must start *inside* the company. Keep the staff informed and involved to keep enthusiasm and interest high. Management must inspire and motivate staff and volunteers at all levels.

- Define the program from its creative idea and benefits to all participants through goals, division of labor, and options for extending, expanding, or ending the effort.

- Assess risks to reputations and resources.

- Define the value of the program and its impact on employees and other stakeholders.

- Partnership agreements should list minimum guarantees as well as the degree of exclusivity each partner will commit to the program.

- Management is a key element of the partnership, requiring skill, experience, and an ability to access outside resources and at the same time assume responsibility for executing the plan and communicating its benefits.

- An evaluation mechanism is important to determine whether the program is reaching its goals and achieving satisfaction for partners and stakeholders.

- A well-managed group of volunteers saves money, enhances commitment, adds talent, and attracts and recruits other volunteers.

- The Internet is a powerful element for broadening and increasing awareness, but it is not the only element. Use technology wisely as part of a total program and stay focused on the cause.

4

Damage Control: Responding to Crises Relating to Your Cause

The picture looked great on paper: a socially responsible company, a respected nonprofit organization, and a partnership of the two entities for the expressed purpose of doing something good. Any part of the mix should be worthy of applause and commendations, together representing an "everybody wins" situation. But alas, it doesn't always work out that way.

McDonald's, of course, is the company that not only changed people's eating habits and literally defined fast food first in the United States and later in cities around the world. It also became one of the first *identity partnerships* by putting its corporate name on Ronald McDonald House, a place that provided temporary housing for families of hospitalized children. The first Ronald McDonald House opened in Philadelphia in 1974. About 25 years later, nearly 200 Ronald McDonald Houses were operational throughout the country. In addition, Ronald McDonald House Charities had awarded more than $200 million in grants to a variety of nonprofit organizations that focused on education and children's health. The company and its program stood as a textbook example of caring, socially responsible marketing, presenting its name, logo, and image where it could be seen doing good for children and families, the market segment that, broad as it is, constitutes McDonald's target.

The company also widely publicized the policy established by its founder, which committed itself to giving something back to each of the communities in which it does business. Apart from taking shots at the nutritional value of McDonald's hamburgers, fries, and fish sandwiches, only the meanest-spirited critics could refrain from praising such a socially conscious, child-friendly corporate leader. Right? Not completely.

Some of the so-called reports were odd, sounding like urban fables. An attack on the company by a minister somewhere in America's Deep South charged that McDonald's was a supporter of the Church of Satan. No evidence was produced to support the charge, but the fact that it was attributed to a reliable source became a matter of some concern to company management. The charge never went far and inflicted no apparent damage to the company's reputation. Despite McDonald's dispatching its representatives to respond to the charge, the company might as well have kept its money in the deep fryer. The story just seemed too unlikely to be taken seriously. Nor was McDonald's armor dented by the protests from nutritional experts, who claimed the fast-food giant was among the worst in the industry when it came to offering healthy items on its menu.

But when the company came under fire from environmental groups that criticized its plastic packaging, McDonald's corporate voice was briefly rendered speechless. The packages were styrofoam and molded plastic and therefore not biodegradable, the critics charged. Worse than just the claim was the fact that McDonald's was chastised for being so successful. That it was the industry leader, highly profitable, and attaching its name to good and charitable causes made it a wide target for critics. McDonald's set the standard for the fast-food business, and because its market was largely children, it should have set a better example and known better, tut-tutted the critics.

McDonald's, however, did not achieve the status it had by falling asleep at the wheel. Before the attacks could gain momentum, the company announced it would work closely with the Environmental Defense Fund to develop alternative, more earth-friendly types of packaging.

Along the way, an important lesson had been noted: No matter how successful a company is, regardless of its business or industry, and in spite of its commitment to being a good corporate citizen, there is always someone nearby who is willing to hate it, if there's a chance the news media will notice. Count on opportunistic special interest organizations targeting that company as their opportunity to advance their own agenda at the company's expense.

Seem harsh? Unfortunately, it's the sad reality of modern business, where a typical budget for the legal department often rivals that of production or marketing. Civilization, particularly in the United States, has become highly litigious. It is big business to create a business for the sole purpose of attacking other businesses, especially industry leaders.

In serving as a countermaneuver to such attacks, cause marketing, certainly not primarily employed for such purposes, is nonetheless a good defense against special interest groups' attack practices and tactics. The rationale is that it would be difficult to effectively attack a company, much less make a negative charge stick, if that company had positioned itself in a community and around the world as one that had built a reputation for doing well by doing good. Anyway, that's the theory, and it actually does have considerable merit. Yet there are always people who are ready and eager to put a good theory to the test.

In the United States, two instruments are employed with amazing frequency and skill to attack and challenge even the strongest institutions and companies and, without conscience or hesitation, hurl mud at their carefully nurtured reputations. These instruments are *the law* and *the media*. Just when you thought it was safe to do business—and maybe some good works and deeds along the way—the sharks came out.

GOOD GUYS AND BAD GUYS: WHICH IS WHICH?

Shakespeare wrote that "first we kill all the lawyers," and if that didn't scare them enough, the *New Yorker* published an entire cartoon book lampooning the profession, while members of the general public seemed to generate an endless supply of lawyer jokes. A spokesperson for the American Bar Association was not amused and said in fact that people should stop the jokes and the disrespect shown to lawyers because it was not, well, respectful.

That seemed to make people really howl! Most of the best lawyer jokes, in fact, seemed to be coming from lawyers, who laughed louder than anyone. At the end of the joke, however, the undeserved damage and outrageous expenses inflicted on so many companies was no laughing matter.

In truth, most people understand that lawyers are necessary to protect the rights, liberties, and freedom of all, but five factors, in particular, have contributed to the public image of lawyers—even so-called good guys—as hired guns who will sue anyone for anything. These factors are (1) huge fees; (2) the fact that America has the highest ratio of lawyers to citizens of any country in the world; (3) the enormous number of frivolous lawsuits filed each year; (4) the growing practice of lawyers trying their cases in the media when lack of substance makes it obvious they would not prevail in court; and (5) book, television, and movie deals routinely negotiated by lawyers on behalf of their clients and themselves as a way of profiting from often tragic situations, frequently at the additional expense of victims.

Simply put, the public's regard for lawyers and the law has been diminished as high-profile lawyers have stretched the limits of ethics and conduct while attacking the reputations of both individuals and corporations. Some people, particularly lawyers, say this description is unfair and too general. But when bad things happen to good companies, it is often the result of lawyers taking a major role in the strategy and tactics, using legal actions as instruments solely aimed at making the evening news, the morning paper, and a big publicity splash.

But the unethical publicity-seeking lawyers could not do it alone. They need a place to take their stories and, conveniently, there are a growing number of outlets desperate for stories to write, show, and tell.

Of course, it is unfair to paint with a broad brush. Certainly, much of the media are honest, accurate, thorough in their reporting, and disinclined to stoop to cheap sensationalism at the expense of some person's or company's reputation. Then again, there is that intense competition, and it's no revelation that bad news attracts a larger audience than good news. The result is a proliferation of tabloid papers and television programs that increasingly say or write anything, feeling somewhat honorable if the charge is clearly identified as an "unconfirmed report" attributed to an "unnamed source."

The media is the all-encompassing term for newspapers, TV and radio stations and networks, cable companies, reporters, editors, broadcasters, producers, packagers, announcers—scapegoats and demons—who are routinely accused of blurring the lines between information and sensationalism, misinformation and education, objectivity and bias, fact and opinion, law and commerce, good and evil. The charges are often unfair, but sometimes they're not.

It is easy to forget that *media* is a plural word that includes such highly respected news sources as the *Christian Science Monitor* and the *Wall Street Journal* as well as tabloid tattlers and Internet gadflies. Veteran news reporter Helen Thomas lamented to the cable network C-SPAN that today anyone with a personal computer and a modem can call himself or herself a publisher and be taken seriously in the wildly competitive rush to be first with a breaking news story and worry about its accuracy or fairness later (if at all). Clearly, respect for the media has declined in the period since CBS News anchorman Walter Cronkite was voted "the most trusted man in America" in a national poll.

On an average day, politicians, business leaders, prominent citizens, and ordinary people tell researchers they believe the media distort news and give favored treatment to causes and people with whom their management agrees politically. Of interest is that the overall opinion that the media are routinely unfair comes from people on the political right and left as well as from many members of the media themselves.

It is against this backdrop that marketers in the 21st century must conduct their business, much of which is with the media. Competitors don't simply compete in the marketplace; they launch expensive, high-profile campaigns of negative ads and sue to block deals and control territories.

Many companies, large and small, have learned that it is not enough anymore to give the public what it wants; it is just as important to make sure not to rub certain people the wrong way—and not only the powerful elite. Consumers who once just ignored companies, brands, products, and issues they didn't like now regularly sign petitions, write letters to editors, organize boycotts and protests, and aggressively work to eliminate products, programs, and issues with which they disagree. And if those companies are aligned with causes, the causes are likely to be caught in the web as well.

Is this true of *all* consumers and competitors? No. It is, however, true in enough cases that legal costs for businesses have soared, and public relations organizations work as tirelessly to neutralize and respond to negative stories and charges as they do to pitch and place positive stories.

Editors and producers discourage their reporters from doing "softball stories" or "puff pieces" and look for critics and adversaries to be included in most every story, not as much for balance as to raise the levels of drama, controversy, and color.

Consider the example of McDonald's. At one time, those who were not satisfied with the nutritional content of a company's food products or disapproved of its choices in packaging materials would have simply avoided the company and taken their business elsewhere. Now they hold press conferences, circulate petitions, organize letter-writing campaigns, and call on the government to force changes in how companies manage their businesses. Cases such as the following are rampant:

- A customer who spilled a cup of hot McDonald's coffee on herself sued the company for millions of dollars. The story was major news, and much of the press and the public still don't know if the customer was joking. McDonald's paid a lot of money and got exactly the kind of publicity it did *not* want.

- Another McDonald's customer, believing he was treated rudely by a cashier, was said to have sued, charging the company with discrimination.

- Several companies became the object of organized boycotts by special interest groups whose members disagreed with opinions expressed by celebrities who had appeared in the companies' radio commercials.

- Protests were aimed at companies by animal rights groups who objected to conditions under which chickens were kept before being killed and packaged for delivery to supermarkets.

- In Chicago, an Olympic torch bearer encountered demonstrators from People for the Ethical Treatment of Animals (PETA) who were angry that a rodeo event would be part of the year's Olympic games. The demonstrators contended that rodeos subject animals to inhumane treatment, and they sought to disrupt the torch ceremony to bring attention to their own issue and position.

The media covered it all in full—TV, radio, and print.

All partnerships of companies and nonprofit organizations, despite careful research and planning, will not be matches made in heaven. Companies undertaking a cause marketing effort, despite an avowed intention to do good, are no less vulnerable to protests, demonstrations, lawsuits, and criticism than companies carrying on their business activities under normal conditions. Indeed, some groups may well oppose or take issue with a specific cause and see such a program as a prime opportunity to present their opposing points of view.

Rosabeth Moss Kanter, professor of business administration at the Harvard Business School and an advisor to numerous business organizations, notes the existence of

the vulnerabilities both parties encounter when they make a public alliance that becomes a public stand. . . . Each organization is staking its reputation on the performance of the other. When Save the Children partners with Denny's, which was accused of racial bias, they take a risk, just as Denny's does when Save the Children is attacked in the press for the problems with the children its donors ostensibly sponsored. Boeing's airplanes' safety record could appear to be at stake when it uses a sheltered workshop as a supplier. But the significance of these partnerships is that they blend capabilities without losing the distinctiveness of each.

HOW A WORST-CASE SCENARIO BECAME A TRULY WORST CASE

Marketers understand there are no sure things. City Year, for example, a highly successful youth outreach organization and a leader in generating corporate support for the AmeriCorps networks, lists Enron as one of its major cause marketing partners.

After a steady run throughout much of the 1990s as one of the hottest energy trading companies in the United States, Enron subsequently filed the country's largest bankruptcy petition in 2001. The company and its management, as well as former executives, became the subjects of scandal, lawsuits, and congressional investigations and hearings. The experts wanted to determine if the company was grossly mismanaged and had been intentionally misrepresenting its actual worth and value, or if its problems—and possible crimes—were deeper and wider than early investigations may have indicated.

This would definitely qualify as a case of a company in crisis.

Enron was a company that cared about its public face and touted its sense of team spirit and commitment to its people. It invested heavily in building, cultivating, and shaping its image and reputation; supporting high-profile causes; putting its name on public buildings; and promoting itself as a good corporate citizen. If, however, as the story unfolded, its corporate house was not in order, its image and reputation would only temporarily distract public (and legal) attention from problems that neither marketing nor philanthropy, separately or together, could solve.

Here I want to refer to the rule that requires companies that want to be regarded as good companies to actually *be* good companies, not just *look like* good companies. If Enron were in fact a good company and its troubles the result of misunderstanding, how might it have responded to its accusers and critics?

Every presentation on crisis management starts with the admonition to executives to tell the truth. In a case such as Enron's, lawyers would advise that the stakes are so high and legal implications so great that telling the truth is not the issue; it would be better to say nothing at all. That might be sound legal advice, but if the company hopes to ever open for business again, silence is not what the public, employees, or shareholders want to hear. If the company is clean, its management needs to say so—emphatically—and back it up with documents. Show the list of causes to which the company has contributed and tell the people who want to believe it stands for something worthwhile that its good works and deeds over several years far outweigh the problem in which it now finds itself, a problem that, if it exists at all, the company pledges to resolve.

And tell the story to the morning news programs, CNN, the all-news cable channels, talk radio programs, and worldwide TV news magazines. Media experts know the venues and programs that influence and shape public opinion and attitudes.

If, on the other hand, the company has in fact done something wrong, it is appropriate that its executives stay out of sight and let their lawyers make the best deals for them that they can within the law and begin planning for the next management team to come on board with a clean record and a mandate to set the company right.

Unfortunately for Enron, in the early days of its crisis the company's top managers said they were innocent of any wrongdoing. They appeared on interview programs and in public hearings projecting arrogance and presenting explanations that would seem unconvincing coming from low-ranking underlings, much less from executives who held MBAs from the country's finest schools. This seemed to make the situation worse. Similarly, the company's accountants came forward and after collecting millions in fees for their expert advice, essentially claimed they knew nothing of what was going on or of the information they had certified as true.

Sadly, if the executives of both the company and its accounting firm would have allowed the persons responsible for the problems to come forward and take responsibility for their misdeeds or misunderstanding, the two organizations—both of which had histories of doing some things right—might have overcome their difficulties and regained traction. The public has a long history of forgiving those who admit wrongdoing and say they're sorry.

Some crisis management experts would say that it is important that the truth sound like the truth. The process is not a game where someone merely delivers an absurdity, says "That's my story and I'm stickin' to it" and wins the match.

Considering the depth and breadth of the problem and the subsequent media coverage it received, the likelihood of Enron's ever fully distancing itself from the permanent stain of its problem is remote. A good strategy would be for its board (or the bankruptcy trustee) to spin off or sell off the company's viable units that could still function as potential profit centers and operate them under new corporate identities, thereby creating an opportunity for investors to recoup some of their losses, albeit over a considerable period. The spun-off enterprises could conceivably even be reunited under a new holding company at a future date, its connection to the tainted Enron ultimately becoming a distant branch on the family tree. And the new entity could direct a portion of its resources to cause marketing, thereby building a record of good corporate citizenship.

The accounting firm with the illustrious history and distinguished reputation will also likely be forced to reinvent itself, perhaps through merger or acquisition, a practice fairly common to its profession.

Fortunately, this is, as noted, a worst-case situation; not every crisis will be of this magnitude. But everything is relative. Mismanagement, illegal actions, and corporate arrogance can be found in businesses of all sizes, and sponsoring a civic event or engaging in charitable fundraising will not protect such behavior.

It is through such circumstances—at least there seem to be a couple of good headline-grabbing scandals each year—that the public's faith in business is seriously shaken. Cynicism reaches new heights regarding the integrity of business in general and all enterprises with which they would be associated.

"If you haven't noticed, America's corporate image has been scratched up pretty badly lately," says Curt Weeden, president of Corporate Contributions Management Academy in Palm Coast, Florida. "Not so long ago, Max de Pree, former chairman and CEO of Herman Miller, Inc., lamented that he couldn't remember any time in recent history when antibusiness rhetoric had been so strong. Then there's Benjamin Barber, who directs Rutgers University's Walt Whitman Center for Culture and Politics of Democracy. He blasted corporate America for not having an interest 'in the public good.'"

Weeden also cites G. J. Meyer, a noted business author, who claimed that "corporations are alienating large numbers of Americans with their behavior . . . . The only way to change anti-big-business feelings is to change that behavior."

It's been said that those who held America together during World War II have earned the right to be called "the greatest generation." Their children, the baby boomers, were called early on "the me generation." Born at a time of new prosperity, boomers are serious about making their fortunes. Reports indicate the only generation that might match them for selfishness is the one that came after them. In sum:

- It is a time of great cynicism.

- Greenmail and corporate raiding have decimated potentially strong companies that became the subjects of best-selling books on corporate greed.

- Public trust in business, the media, and government is at an all-time low.

- Once prestigious trade groups, such as the American Medical Association, the American Heart Association, and the American Cancer Society have been accused of compromising their integrity by allowing commercial ventures to use their name, logo/seal, and implied endorsement for huge seven-figure and eight-figure fees.

- The media—television, print, and the Internet—routinely present rumors and gossip as facts and overly sensationalize news stories.

- Personal and corporate responsibility seem to have become outmoded ideas as lawyers, the media, and virtually everyone else get blamed for the low approval ratings of most businesses and business leaders.

- Special interest groups are organized to advance their interests, mostly at the expense of corporations. The bigger and more successful the organization, the greater the volume of the attack.

- People who don't like a company, brand, or issue call a news conference, send out a press release, and use the media to exert pressure and control the story.

This would appear to be the worst possible time to launch, build, or manage a business. In an earlier book, *Crisis Marketing: When Bad Things Happen to Good Companies,* I noted that some of the biggest success stories in business took place in what everyone had described as the worst possible time.

The concept of a cause marketing program offers a solid approach to generating awareness and goodwill, establishing or enhancing a corporate image, and promoting a sense of integrity regarding businesses and business leaders, regardless of size, industry, or geography. As McDonald's founder proved many times over, a company that demonstrates a sense of social responsibility and concern for its customers and stakeholders will still be there when shortsighted, self-serving opportunists have fallen away.

In good times, a cause marketing program can be of great benefit to the company, the cause, and the public. It creates a reservoir of goodwill from which the company may need to draw if times get tough. In bad times, the company and nonprofit organization that had consistently maintained positions as good corporate citizens have the support and goodwill of a public that wants them to succeed so they can remain to help another day. In times of crisis, a good reputation and the goodwill of the public can mean the difference between survival and complete collapse.

You are now ready to check off the steps you took in preparing your cause marketing program. You have:

- Created a partnership between the company and a nonprofit organization

- Written a defined statement of purpose with a commitment to a cause

- Prepared a clear and succinct marketing plan (with a situation analysis, objectives, strategy and tactics, timeline, and budget)

- Assigned management roles and responsibilities

- Established mechanisms for communicating effectively with key centers of influence, such as employees, customers, appropriate legal and regulatory agents, and other stakeholders

Having completed these preparations, your well-organized cause marketing program is now ready to go public.

Almost.

PLAN FOR CRISIS MARKETING

A frequently overlooked (until it is needed) part of most marketing plans is a contingency procedure for dealing with worst-case scenarios—that is, a crisis marketing plan.

In business, *crisis* is a relative term that can describe any number of occurrences that greatly impact a company. From scandals in the corporate board room to strikes, hostile takeovers, product tampering, or recalls—or a phone call from the producer of *60 Minutes* announcing he'd like to drop by—a crisis can take many forms.

Think Ford and Firestone in the summer of 2000, when faulty tires were said to be responsible for hundreds of disasters involving Ford vehicles. Or the lead story in the news media of the airline or plane manufacturer, whose planes were found to have a higher-than-usual percentage of tragic problems. Or the tabloid television show report that insisted people were not safe at a particular hotel chain, basing the damaging statement on an inspection of only one of the chain's 3,000 properties. These may be extreme cases but are real situations that could occur at virtually any company in any industry.

A crisis affecting a cause marketing program might be a financial scandal (e.g., when United Way's top executive was found to have diverted funds for his personal use); a financial problem of another sort, such as the corporate side of a partnership filing bankruptcy without warning (as Enron did at a time when it was engaged in cause marketing partnerships with a number of high-profile groups from the Boys & Girls Clubs to the Houston Ballet); the resignation under pressure of a CEO or program manager (e.g., when the head of the American Red Cross was forced to leave following criticism of her decision to allocate funds for matters other than those contributors understood would be their purpose); pressure from special interest groups over working conditions, use of unskilled laborers, or failure to file the correct government reporting forms.

The scandal could be a big deal or relatively inconsequential, but it nonetheless sends lawyers filing suits or demanding disclosure, spokespersons racing to microphones and cameras, and the media reporting that the company and the nonprofit organization partnered in an effort to do something good and worthy had come under suspicion of maybe not being so good after all.

There is no sure way to keep societal influences and human nature from throwing your best laid plans a curve, but there are steps you can take that constitute reasonable measures in damage control.

Things to Do before You're in Trouble

Once a crisis situation becomes public knowledge, almost any actions are (and are viewed as) *re*actions and are often discounted as such. The best crisis management initiatives are those put in place *before* a troublesome situation occurs. Because it is seldom possible to control when problems will arise, a strong argument can be made for not putting off crisis management initiatives until the next budget year or when the new CEO comes on board or the Chicago Cubs win a World Series. Start now.

Before a crisis is upon you, begin to create a reservoir from which the company can draw. The basic steps are these:

- Generate publicity: get your story out.

- Tell your story early and often; don't just issue a press release, assume it did the trick, and wait for the phone to ring.

- Don't let bad news be the first time the public reads or hears about your company.

- Be honest in what you say and how you say it; changing public opinion becomes more difficult if you are already distrusted.

Publicity. This is regarded as getting a company, organization, or brand name "out there," increasing awareness and visibility. It is that, but so is advertising. The major distinction after cost (a good advertising schedule in most markets can be quite costly) is that a story publicized through mainstream media makes an impression and often gets a stamp of credibility that comes with placements the audience knows were not paid for.

When a local television station, or newspaper, network or cable show, or national magazine refers to a company as *hot, new and noteworthy, old and solid, a leader, a good corporate citizen, one of the best employers in the industry,* or other positive term, the audience or target market not only sees the reference but, it's hoped, remembers it. In addition, a good story (or a bad story for that matter) goes into media databases and will likely be used for background material or research as other reporters and producers search for information on the company.

With all due respect to hardworking members of the press, most of what is reported in the media is not the result of reporters' digging but of publicists' bringing story material to reporters and editors. When a pitched idea is accepted and used, other members of the media are among the first to notice it. "A company to watch" *becomes* a company to watch after such a designation is reported and attributed to a source acknowledged by the media.

In good times, the first step in getting your story to the media is to get your story to the media. Don't wait for reporters to come to you. The media are pitched hundreds of stories each week. Even if your story was accidently noticed and a reporter, editor, or producer wanted to use it, he or she would first have to get to you through a sea of press releases, backgrounders, fact sheets, media kits, photographs, demo disks, and promotional items covered in the logos of other companies. Like the "killer Web site" that no one ever saw because no one had been told of its existence or how to find it, a company's message must be delivered or it will never reach its intended destination.

A great deal of corporate arrogance is evident, with executives continually railing at PR reps because the media are not paying enough attention to the company. That isn't how the system works. It's not the job of the press to search out someone who thinks he or she has a story worth telling. On any given day, management at even the most successful companies are furious at their PR people because the company was not mentioned in a story in that day's edition of the *Wall Street Journal* or a competitor got the cover of *Forbes* or *Business Week*. These were most likely stories the competition went after and got.

Tell your story early and often. Highlight your story's uniqueness and the benefits of what you do. Note: Even benefits that sound familiar are still reasons why your public should care what

you do. To make a supportable claim of low cost or high performance is to provide information that good editors and reporters
are not supposed to ignore, even if it's not front-page material.
Remember that claims of low cost and high quality are a lot more
persuasive when accompanied by comparison numbers that vali-
date the claim.

*Don't let bad news be the first news the public sees or hears about
your company.* This point can't be overstated. Too many companies think they have as much time as they want or need to accomplish their objectives, but crisis situations rarely give warnings that
they are about to occur. If the public or the media first become
aware of your company because of its involvement in a negative
story, negativity will be a first impression that will likely color the
company's image for a long time to come.

If the company has been late getting started in generating positive news items or a well-orchestrated media relations program, a
cause marketing effort is a good place to begin. If the public's first
exposure to a company is a report of the company's doing something good for the community, that's a good try at making a positive
first impression. If the company is already well (or even slightly)
known, news of its participation in a cause marketing effort is still
likely to be well received, ideally enhancing its reputation and winning respect.

Be honest. In an era of intense media scrutiny and competition,
there is an eagerness to dig below the surface and look for stories
behind the stories. As the public is learning more about your company, it is advisable that information not be formed on a foundation
of exaggeration and hype. To be caught in a web of misstatements
undermines credibility and invites suspicion. Remember that cause
marketing is about benefiting from *actually* doing good works.

IN A CRISIS: DAMAGE CONTROL NOW

As a crisis situation unfolds, it is essential to *take the lead* in defining the substance and tone of the story. Some marketers view a crisis as an opportunity—to exploit a timely interest in the company as well as to show that the company and its management have "the right stuff" and deserve support.

The four essential points of effective crisis management are:

1. Designate a single, credible spokesperson to tell your story.

2. Get your story out *first.*

3. Position your company and cause in a larger context than the crisis.

4. Communicate—especially keeping your own people informed.

These points appear to be extremely simple. They are. They have also proved to be very effective in countless situations. Yet perhaps some companies or organizations regard them as too simple, because when they are not the basis of the strategy the company follows, crises have been known to escalate and turn into even worse situations. Some companies, in the words of songwriter Paul Simon, "think too much" and concoct explanations of what went wrong that defy logic or believability. It might be said that this is not a time for creativity. Simple, direct, concise statements of facts that can be verified—for better or worse—will position the company more favorably than implausible, convoluted attempts at justification or legal interpretations.

Designate a single, credible person to tell your story. The single designated spokesperson should be an experienced public relations specialist from the company staff, the cause marketing program staff, or an outside agency. The designated spokesperson should not be the organization's CEO or legal counsel. The PR representative can prepare concise remarks documented in written handouts for accuracy, can anticipate tough questions and prepare satisfactory responses, and while being direct and forthcoming, can say when necessary, "I don't know, but I will get that information to you."

A spokesperson is not required or expected to have answers to every question, but a CEO is. Every time a top executive can't or won't respond to a question, it can be interpreted as a sign of unwillingness to say something that could be damaging or as a lack of knowledge about what is going on in his or her organization. Neither is usually a helpful impression to convey.

A representative can buy time to frame a satisfactory response. This is *spin,* a word that some people consider to mean lying or deliberately misleading. It's not. Spin is presenting information in ways that emphasize the positive and minimize the negative connotations and implications of comments. When the process crosses the line and becomes untruthful or misleading, it is no longer spin; then it is lying. It's not really complicated and not a gray area. Spin is an artful process that has been employed by communications and marketing professionals for decades.

This book may seem excessively hard on lawyers, but there are lawyers who practice law and there are lawyers who manage strategies in ways that may win legal decisions but leave the image and reputation of the company or person tarnished and forever under suspicion of having gotten away with wrongdoing by manipulating a system or process.

Lawyers who practice law are good. Lawyers who refuse to respond to media or public inquiries or, worse, issue a terse "no comment" are not friends of the crisis management process. Because few issues are all right or all wrong, pure good or pure evil, the issue does not have to be to invoke the law as a shield, say too much and inflame, or concede an already dangerous situation. Most experienced, skilled public relations professionals are aware of legal pitfalls or know when to consult with legal professionals to correctly frame a response or statement that will not make a situation worse.

Having a single designated spokesperson also avoids the likelihood of conflicting comments or statements leading to misunderstanding.

Get your story out first. Getting your story out first is a consideration that can affect the entire tone of the crisis for as long as it lasts and affect even how the organization will be regarded when the matter is long over.

If a member of the media discovers (or receives information from a source) that a company, nonprofit organization, or cause partnership has a problem, the subject is forced to respond. Responses have historically been interpreted as defensive, angry, hostile, or any number of other emotional colorations that do not show the subject at its best. There are times when this cannot be helped—when the leadership was truly unaware of a problem until it blew wide open and everyone learned of it at the same time. In such situations, again a public relations professional skilled in crisis management can likely help frame a statement or response that suggests candor and a determination to correct improprieties or other problems quickly.

If, on the other hand, the leadership did have information, a suspicion, or even a suggestion that a crisis could be in the making, to begin positioning for such a possibility is critical. In such situations, the question is always to speak up or not to speak up. Some organizations choose not to speak up, hoping the problem can be corrected without anyone ever knowing about it. It might be possible to "dodge the bullet" and actually have something of crisis proportions resolved without the public, the media, shareholders, employees, regulators, or anyone else ever knowing about it. It could happen.

Experienced crisis managers rarely recommend not speaking up. The risks are usually far too great, and the crisis then escalates from its original problem to include attempts to conceal information that could have helped everyone cut their losses. Even if the problem doesn't include criminal activity, the company's or organization's reputation and integrity risk being forever called into question. Any stories written or told about the company are far more likely to refer to both the company's past problems and its attempts to cover up those problems. Such descriptions are usually not helpful in an organization's efforts to recruit top talent, secure regulatory approvals, or attract investors.

The recommended approach to damage control has the company as the bearer of its own bad news – being out front first with the story.

Sometimes perhaps all that can be said at the time is that the company, organization, or partnership has learned a situation may exist that bears investigation and study. The spokesperson can add: "As information becomes available, we will share what we know in an effort to create an accurate record." Such a simple declaration is a first step in taking charge of an issue, positioning the company as aware, concerned, and serious rather than appearing to be defensive, confused, or disconnected. As information becomes available, its presentation may be easier to manage (depending, of course, on how bad the bad news proves to be). Even if the information is bad in the extreme, however, the company will have, to its credit, the fact that it broke the story itself as a sign of its continuing competence and integrity.

Not all crisis situations are of a type that marketers can solve, even with the help of a highly skilled and experienced team. Normally, however, it is the marketing department in an organization that oversees and manages the communication functions and therefore, even in the most dicey legal situations, marketers can provide expertise that can be enormously beneficial in developing a crisis management strategy.

Very often in crisis situations the first inclination of management is to cover the corporate flanks by turning to the legal department or to outside legal counsel. In worst-case situations, perhaps including illegal or criminal activities, the outcome will not be determined by marketing. But as most crises require someone having a finger on the pulse of public opinion and an eye toward how the company will keep the flag waving, with its image and reputation on the line, aspects of the crisis do indeed become marketing problems.

The marketing team has invested itself in developing relationships with members of the media and in positioning the company. As such, marketing should have a major role in crisis management, much of which is a communications function—and therein lies marketing's strength.

Positioning your company and cause.   Positioning the company and the cause in a larger context than the crisis is essential. A company, organization, or partnership with a history of service and integrity (or at least free of scandal) has something to draw on: the number of employees or volunteers who gave something back to the community; the many people who benefited from programs in which the company or its partners made contributions; and perhaps awards and other types of recognition. This is the time to talk about all of these.

An *ongoing publicity program* increases the likelihood that the first news the public hears about the company won't be that the company is in trouble. Past years' business activities, even if relatively uneventful, should be exploited. They were, after all, normal productive years of untainted business activity. Such a history allows the spokesperson to say that the company has never experienced trouble worth noting in its [fill in the number of years] history.

The message that must be advanced is that the company or organization should not be judged or regarded badly based on what is for it—placed in the larger context—an unusual situation. This is an example of using the reservoir of goodwill the company should have been building since its inception. If no such reservoir exists, create one by going back in the archives of the company and the organization's history to list anything it might have done to benefit the community and beyond.

"Better late than never" is not a marketing expression, but if it's all you've got to work with at the time, use it.

Communicate. Public relations professionals like to point out that a company or organization has many publics. These are people who have their own reasons for wanting to know what the company has done, when, and why. Tell your story to each of these publics in ways that highlight what is most important to them, but tell it first to the people closest to you—the company's, organization's, or partnership's employees and volunteers along with other stakeholders. These are people with a particular interest in the survival and success of the program. They deserve to learn the details of what the crisis situation means from you rather than learning about it from media reports or, worse, from a friend or family member who heard it from someone else.

Employees, volunteers, and other stakeholders comprise a constituency that wants to be on your side. They are invested, either financially or emotionally, and may have something significant at risk if the company or the cause falls from favor with the public. Give them a reason to remain loyal and to continue their support. If the crisis is of such a proportion that it will result in major damage, again it is best that your constituency learn of it from you and not from the grapevine.

TAKING THE HIT

Damage control is not about changing the facts of a situation. Facts are what they are. Companies, like people, are judged by how they respond to difficult situations. Consider the more common expressions used to describe behavior in times of crisis: *courageous, mature, honest, responsible, noble, decent* rather than untrustworthy, self-serving, irresponsible, buck passing.

Sometimes companies or organizations get into trouble because someone has simply done something, intentionally or inadvertently, that should not have been done. The subsequent crisis could be allegations of fraud or other illegal activity, or it may be only a harsh publicity offensive initiated by special interest groups that don't like your company or your cause. Obviously, the nature and extent of the problem will be a major factor in determining what will need to be done when the crisis is over.

If a bad thing happens to a good company, the public has a long history of forgiving. At various times major corporations (Ford, Exxon, Disney, Procter & Gamble) and well-known cause-related organizations (United Way, Save the Children, UNICEF, the Red Cross) have come under fire or been rocked by scandal. Many observers thought some of them would not survive. So far, they have. If the company's or program's response to a crisis is well considered and well managed, confidence and respect can be maintained or restored.

Lies are remembered. Arrogance and ingratitude are remembered. What may appear to be absurdly simplistic is well documented. Thus, when a company, organization, or a cause is in trouble, remember that:

- People typically accept an honest explanation of the situation or problem.

- People want to see someone take charge, take responsibility for what happened, and be available to reassure them and answer any lingering questions.

- If necessary, people want and expect an apology and a promise to make reparations or compensate for losses.

- People want a promise that problems will not go uncorrected and an assurance that it will not happen again.

It is unfortunate that pressure groups and special interest organizations are so abundant. For every committee organized for virtually any purpose, a "counter" group (sometimes with an impressive name but with only one member) seems to exist as well. For companies and nonprofits that form a partnership to work on behalf of good causes, it is reasonable to expect adversarial groups to form in response to such efforts and emotions on both sides to run high. Critics and adversarial groups have become sophisticated in their manipulation of the media and the legal system. Whether or not it is appropriate (or worth it) to mount a counterstrategy, it is important to at least understand your adversaries' arguments.

On the positive side, much of the public seems to be on to what's happening. The proliferation of cable news channels and programs that feature people of opposing views shouting at one another on virtually any subject has resulted in the public's tuning out the name calling and groundless accusations and weighing information selectively.

Many people automatically view what the media deliver to them with a degree of suspicion. Although such cynicism is unfortunate, many good organizations (and people) have survived because the public refused to accept baseless charges and rumors as facts, waiting to hear the other side of the story and extending the benefit of doubt.

And cause marketers continue to do well by doing good.

S U M M A R Y

- A growing type of business is one that exists for the purpose of attacking other businesses.

- Cause marketing—participating in an effort to do good—is a useful defensive strategy that builds public goodwill and often frustrates critics.

- The artful manipulation of lawsuits and the media by special interest groups is increasingly becoming the most commonly used instrument to attack companies and causes.

- Because companies undertaking cause marketing programs should anticipate criticism and attacks, they should develop an outline for damage control and recognize early on the need for possible crisis management.

- Public trust in both business and the media is at perhaps an all-time low. Cause marketing can help restore dignity, integrity, and generosity to the business landscape.

- The media routinely present rumors and unconfirmed information in an effort to be first with a big story. Anticipate worst-case scenarios and be prepared to preempt an attack or respond.

- Honesty, accessibility, and effective communication skills are essential elements of a crisis management plan.

- Publicizing efforts early helps create a reservoir of goodwill a company or cause marketing program can draw on in a crisis.

- Don't let critics or adversaries define and control your difficulties or crises. Be first to tell the extent of your problems.

- Communicate details of a crisis directly and early to your employees, volunteers, and other stakeholders and enlist their support.

- Present the company and the cause in a larger context than the crisis. Tell what good actions have come before and position the crisis as one dark episode among many bright events.

- The public is far more likely to forgive companies that get into trouble if the companies are honest, take responsibility, and say they will correct their mistakes.

- A company's or cause's constituency wants to continue to believe in and support it but needs to be given a reason. The marketing people usually are charged with communicating that reason to them.

5

September 11, 2001

Some business crises can be anticipated. It is unfortunate, but pragmatic executives expect some misfortune to occur that will trigger unwanted events—perhaps forced plant closings, product recalls, or a boardroom scandal that could conceivably send the company's stock into a free fall. No one, however, could have foreseen the shock or prolonged trauma that would follow the terrorist attacks on the United States on September 11, 2001.

Terrorism was of course not unknown to the strongest economic and military power on earth. Americans had witnessed attacks before in New York and Oklahoma City, on luxury cruise ships, and at military bases around the world. But on a quiet weekday morning, as Americans went off to work and school and sipped coffee at home, watching *The Today Show* and *Good Morning America,* terrorists hijacked U.S. jetliners and crashed them into a field in Pennsylvania, the Pentagon in Washington, and, most dramatically as the world watched in stunned disbelief on live television, the World Trade Center's twin towers in downtown Manhattan, the heart of the nation's financial center.

The towers collapsed into rubble, thousands of people were killed, and downtown New York City became a great cloud of black smoke that would linger for weeks. Across the United States the psychological effects would last much longer. In the days following the attacks, much of American business and industry came to a virtual halt, with ambitious marketing programs and promotions put on hold. All air and rail traffic stopped. Television and radio programming on all channels and stations became 24-hour news reports. Entertainment and sports events were canceled or rescheduled. Broadcast and cable media, for the most part, did not run commercial spots, in some instances because of contractual stipulations and in other cases as a judgment call. Reports and scenes of devastation and destruction hardly provided a favorable backdrop to sponsors' messages, regardless of the products. People united.

Gradually, many marketers and much of the public sensed more than a slight change in the environment. No one knew how it would evolve or what direction it would take, but it was clear that much was different. The ads, the programs, the events, the conversations all reflected the change; there was a death in the family. Many in business, the arts, and the public sector had seen the effects of terrorism before, but now there was a sense that, to borrow a line from the action movies, "this time, it's personal."

In the midst of grief and tragedy, businesses still had to open each day and life had to go on. For marketers, to present new campaigns and promotions with the usual accompanying fireworks and excitement seemed very much out of place. That was not the mood of the market.

In addition, each day's economic news reported business closings, layoffs, and job cuts that had begun months before the terrorists' attacks defined the market climate. It was against this landscape that marketers arrived for work, forced to rethink plans that might have been in development for months or longer.

Whether because of the uncertainties of the economy, the tragic events of September 11, or the existence of a state of war, one thing was clear: Virtually every business and profession in the United States, at least temporarily, put aside its marketing plan and began reexamining its commitments and strategies. It was clear that the next wave of marketing activity would have to include more than a sensitive poem or tribute presented as a full-page ad above a company's logo in a national newspaper. The billboards, decals, and window signs announcing support for firefighters, police, and the country itself were once considered knee-jerk reactions, not marketing.

Marketers identify opportunities, often those that come about from unlikely occasions and sources. Crisis marketing considers what opportunities can be created from the most threatening, damaging, or unfavorable situations. And this one certainly qualified.

But how does a company sell a new car, a restaurant franchise, a computer game, or designer dresses or launch a new fragrance or present a new line of exciting creations to a public that has never felt less like buying or celebrating and even admitted feeling guilty if it started to feel happy?

To say that coming back in such a market is a challenge seems an understatement, but survivors of past wars, recessions, business closings, and setbacks remember that head shaking and resigned groaning don't help the turnaround effort; they only hasten the end.

Not long ago Chairman Alan Greenspan of the Federal Reserve Bank used the phrase "irrational exuberance" to describe the dot-com frenzy of soaring stock market gains for unproven companies. That seems like a century ago. In September of 2001, the opposite was true; businesses operated in an environment of real and quite understandable fear and uncertainty. The lesson to be learned is about cycles, ups and downs, the next phase—whatever we choose to call it. Time is not standing still, and about the only sure thing that can be counted on at the end of each business day is that another business day will begin a few hours later.

The bravado and unbridled displays of patriotism that followed the September 11 attacks served a useful purpose as part of the healing and uniting process, repairing the psychological damage to businesses. But a *plan,* with clearly defined objectives, strategy, tactics, and budget, is what would be needed when the decals begin to get a little used.

What gets the attention of the marketplace is an approach that reflects *creativity,* a word that is heard less and less in too many marketing programs. Taking an imaginative and innovative approach to presenting the company's or cause's message is the marketer's basic skill. It is not doing what all the other guys seem to be doing, and the message will be remembered.

Correctly positioning a product, brand, company, or cause is essential in the best of times; doing so in a crisis climate is an absolute requirement. The public makes its choices based on price, quality, value, image, and integrity, though not necessarily in that order. People like to know they can trust the people they choose to support with their dollars and their loyalty. For some businesses, there may be no second chances.

OPPORTUNISM OR A CHANGE OF HEART?

September 11, 2001, became a marker in history, a dividing line of before and after. A phrase that has become commonplace is "in the wake of 9/11," always followed by an example of how life in much of the world was changed by events of that day.

Once again the adage proved true that tragedy brings out the best and the worst in people. The media managed to capture much of both. With so much destruction of commercial sites in downtown Manhattan, what followed was the inevitable looting of retail businesses, commonplace after riots and celebrations in streets where businesses were left unattended. Phony telemarketers called people to solicit funds for victims of the tragedy in what were quickly identified as hastily conceived cons. News of such occurrences fueled the mood of cynicism that had already become the prevailing sense of certain age and demographic groups.

But on the other end of the spectrum were the individuals and groups that dropped what they were doing and rushed to the area, wanting only to help. In addition to thousands of innocent people killed by the terrorists' attacks, hundreds of others—police, fire-fighters, and rescue workers—were killed as buildings collapsed and trapped many who had come to help.

The owners and employees of restaurants threw open their doors to do what they did best. They fed people around the clock without charge, often at personal expense and some risk, as smoke and debris continued to fill the city's downtown and surrounding sections. Rescue workers, city crews, medical personnel, and area residents, many of them dazed and shocked, found friendship, support, and a widening sense of community.

Acts of philanthropy and dramatic demonstrations of social responsibility materialized so quickly, by necessity, that acts of kindness routinely went uncredited, which appeared to be fine with the donors and people who worked tirelessly without apparent thought of reward or recognition. But that would change.

Many businesses and corporations, aware of how funding opportunities, publicity, and images are created, wanted to make certain their concerns and contributions did not go unnoticed. Within days after the terrorists' attacks, commemorative products began appearing, and companies were standing in line to purchase premium space—full-page ads in the highest circulation newspapers in the United States and around the world—to eagerly announce their sympathy, support, and, in some cases, sales.

The national edition of the *New York Times,* read by people thousands of miles from the scene of the New York tragedy, on September 16 carried 18 full-page ads and several pages more of smaller placements, ranging from the touching to the overtly patriotic to the almost obscenely opportunistic. At the paper's open rate, the cost of a single black and white page in the *New York Times* in 2001 was nearly $108,000 (though the paper offered significantly reduced rates to advertisers using the space to memorialize victims of the tragedy).

Many of the advertisers were not regular, frequent, or even occasional advertisers. Some were companies that had not previously found a need to position themselves as especially interested in being advocates for victims of life's misfortunes. Clearly, some had tested the winds and identified what might well be, while tragic, the public relations opportunity of a lifetime.

Some of the messages were dignified; some were imaginative; some prompted people across the land to ask out loud, "What could they have been thinking?" Was this good corporate citizenship? Was it cause marketing? Was it any kind of marketing at all? A sampling of the sentiments:

- Kmart's full-page ad carried a color rendering of an American flag that readers of the paper were asked to cut out and display in their windows in support of America. The retailer's name appeared discreetly in the lower corner of the page.

- Prudential Financial's full-page ad carried the words to *God Bless America*.

- A page in which "The People of Puerto Rico" expressed sympathy for the people of New York seemed thoughtful but curious.

- Full-page ads in which General Motors, A&P Supermarkets, and Sears each urged the public to support the American Red Cross were light on text and graphics but focused on message.

- Ethan Allen Interiors, Cushman & Wakefield Property Management, the Allianz Group, Merrill Lynch, Aon, Staples, Bloomingdale's, Lord & Taylor, and American Express Financial Advisors were each represented with a dignified and understated full-page ad offering patriotic messages of support or prayers for the families of victims.

- Home Depot's full-page ad urged people to bring their tax refund checks to a collection point in each of its stores, presumably with the money to be used to help in the relief and rescue effort.

- J&R Music World/Computer World delivered a heartfelt message of sympathy in a full-page ad, followed by the company's logo and the announcement, "No charge for shipping in the New York and New Jersey metropolitan area at the present time." (Huh?)

A week after September 11th, more companies were getting the idea. Ads, signs, buttons, banners, and commemorative displays were everywhere. The marketing effort was by no means confined to newspaper ads. Sentiments spilled over into TV advertising, the home pages of most corporate Web sites, point-of-sale displays, and e-mails by the millions. This is not to suggest, however, that the newspaper ads had abated. With logos blazing, another dozen or so full-page ads in the national edition of the *New York Times* carried messages that were alternately humble and nationalistic, reflecting sadness and grief, and expressing condolences, tributes, and wishes for prayers and peace. Others, self-serving and opportunistic, seemed to think a national period of sadness was a good time for a sale:

- Morrell & Company announced in a full-page ad that it would hold a "Grapes of Grief and Gratitude" benefit wine auction for families of New York firefighters, police, and emergency response professionals.

- The American International Group's full-page ad used its space to praise itself for working around the clock but failed to mention what the American International Group is or does.

- A New York attorney bought a full-page ad directed "To Members of Congress," urging that passengers on United Flight 93 be considered for the Congressional Medal of Honor.

- AOL Time Warner's ad asked readers to join with it in supporting the September 11 Fund, the American Red Cross, and five other named charities.

- The New York Times Company itself took a page in its paper to announce it had established a fund of its own to help victims' families.

- The Metropolitan Transit Authority, Air Transportation Association, Banc of America Securities, Royal Embassy of Saudi Arabia, and the Port Authority of New York and New Jersey each ran full-page ads.

For days to come, dozens of costly national edition full-page ads continued to appear, some of them becoming more creative, others simply curious by their presence. Most of the ads had the look of sponsorship ads in yearbooks, theater programs, and testimonial dinner fundraisers.

No one seemed able to recall when a terrorist attack on a major city seemed to prompt such an enormous wave of corporate-image marketing in the past. Weighing in with full-page ads in the *Times* were:

- The Greater Fort Lauderdale Convention and Visitors Bureau

- The Commonwealth of the Bahamas

- The People of Berlin (signed by nine dignitaries)

- The Greater Miami Convention and Visitors Bureau

- Los Angeles Convention and Visitors Bureau

- The Republic of Lebanon

- Greek Orthodox Church

- St Paul Fire and Marine Life Insurance Company

- Pfizer

- United States Tennis Association

- Lehman Brothers

- Verizon

and in some cleverly crafted messages with a sense of demographic awareness were:

- The *New York Times* took out a second full-page ad within its pages to print this line from a song by the late John Lennon: "Imagine all the people, living life in peace."

- Starbucks' full-page color ad for its 30th anniversary incorporated a paragraph, prominently set off in bold italics, noting it had contributed $1 million to the September 11 Fund. A few weeks later the company took out a second full page. Above the fold was only the headline "No gift reaches so far and wide as a helping hand." Below the fold was this copy, set out in open text on a white background without illustration:

    Thank you to our customers and partners for giving so generously to the Starbucks Care Fund. Beginning with Starbucks' initial contribution of $1.2 million, a total of $2.5 million has been raised so far for the United Way September 11th Fund, which will help to provide much needed assistance to the victims, their families and all those affected by the tragic events of September 11th. And a special thank you to our employee partners who have donated more than 750,000 cups of hot coffee for relief efforts in New York City, Washington, D.C. and Central Pennsylvania.

The $3.7 million was significant. Add to that the free coffee (an average small cup of Starbucks coffee sells for around $3 . . . times 750,000), and one had to be impressed.

- ABC Carpet & Home stores printed a letter from author and self-help guru Deepak Chopra reflecting on family, fear, and vulnerability in a sensitively presented full-page ad in the *Times* that was repeated in several other editions.

- A Toys "R" Us ad used a color drawing of an American flag as if drawn by a child using crayons on the upper half of a page. Below the fold, the ad copy read "Let your kids show their true colors. Make a Flag. Make a Difference. September 27–30." The ad included the message to "bring your kids to Toys "R" Us or Kids "R" Us to make an American flag. All materials are available in the store for free." The store said it would donate $1 on behalf of each participating child to the Toys "R" Us Children's Fund "9/11 Emergency Relief Fund," which had been newly established to be "used for scholarships, counseling and other support systems in place for children and families affected by the September 11th tragedy."

- In a text-heavy (when compared to other ads appearing on this subject) quarter-page *New York Times* ad, the Wildlife Conservation Society extended its sympathy, thoughts, and prayers and, in honor of one of its lost employees, said it would "donate to the recovery and relief effort all gate proceeds received on Saturday, September 29, at our five wildlife parks, the Bronx Zoo, the New York Aquarium, and the Central Park, Prospect Park and Queens Zoos." In the next paragraph of the same ad, the organization noted that "the day after Thanksgiving, we will provide complimentary admission to all area residents at the opening night of our annual Bronx Zoo Holiday Lights show."

- America's Second Harvest, in a full-page ad that began: "America's Second Harvest and our affiliates would like to thank our food industry partners for their generosity in helping to serve the rescue workers and others affected by the events in New York City and Washington, D.C. during the last month." The ad, using blue and red inks, then went on to thank more than 130 food companies and other enterprises, from Acirca to Yoo-Hoo Chocolate Beverage Company. The list included trade unions, hospitals, warehouses, and technology companies, among many others. The ad concluded with a "thank you" to the listed enterprises that "brought much relief to many during this difficult time, as you do to hungry Americans all year long."

■ Sensa Pens, in promotional material directed to its dealer network, offered a specially designed red, white, and blue "United We Stand" Sensa Pen and pledged "100% of the manufacturer's net profits to the United Way September 11 Fund." Previously, the company had marketed "The World's Most Comfortable Pen" in a promotion to benefit the Healing Hands Project of the Healing Hands Foundation.

■ On September 30, the *Chicago Tribune* ran a full-page ad in color against a soft background of patriotic imagery. Its headline: "We are forever changed. But our uniquely American ability to put aside our differences for the common good is still intact. As is our overwhelming generosity." The copy noted that the Tribune Disaster Relief Fund and its McCormick Tribune Foundation had raised more than $5 million, and with the matching funds from the Foundation, more than $7.5 million was available for disaster relief for "organizations serving those who need it most."

■ On television and in print ads, several automobile companies declared that terrorists should be sent a message that they could not keep America down . . . therefore, buying a new car was an act of patriotism, sort of. Both Ford and GM seemed to be testing the limits of flag waving.

■ Discover Card launched an ad campaign that promised "Every time you use your Discover Card, we'll make a donation to America's relief efforts, until we reach our goal of 5 million

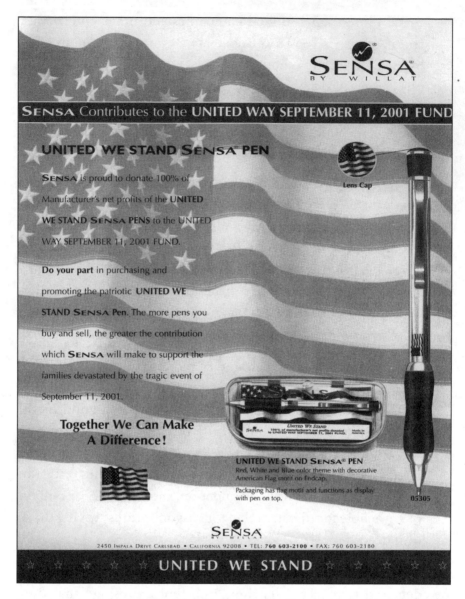

Sensa pens created a special edition "United We Stand" American flag-theme pen with 100 percent of the company's profits going to the United Way September 11 Fund. The company reported demand was overwhelming, as the public sought a way to contribute to a victims' relief fund and, at the same time, retain a simple, tasteful memento of an important moment in history. In an earlier cause marketing effort, Sensa donated proceeds from product sales to the Healing Hands Project of the Healing Hands Foundation. (Courtesy of Sensa by Willat. Used with permission.)

dollars. Just by doing what you do every day, you can help the families and victims of September 11th." The ad concluded with an offer to get a "Discover America Flag Card."

As corporate America was incorporating the flag into a seemingly infinite number of ad layouts, the entertainment industry wanted to help as well. Concerts were organized, literary readings were held, and telethons scheduled. One such event brought together a number of rock music superstars for a concert/television special/CD/DVD. The sponsors of the event—Bear Stearns, eBay, Ford, PepsiCo, Vivendi Universal, and SoundView Technology Group—each contributed at least $1 million to underwrite the event; Sony's Columbia Records paid $1 million for the rights to record the concert and said it would donate a portion of its income from the sales of CDs and DVDs to the Robin Hood Foundation, a New York City charity.

Country music stars, Broadway stage performers, soul music acts, and others presented their own stage/CD/video fundraising events. Everyone wanted to do something "in the wake of 9/11," to stand up and be counted as a company or an individual and become part of something bigger, more important, patriotic, respectful, and respectable.

If cause marketing is behaving in a socially responsible manner and putting company resources to work for the benefit of the community, then a new majority of businesses were wildly eager to demonstrate their cause marketing. Then again, if an important rule of cause marketing is to not permit your motives to appear to be self-serving, then some practitioners were clearly behind the curve, overtly attempting to seize the moment to garner publicity, recognition, cash, and perhaps an award or two.

Bob Garfield wrote in *Advertising Age:* "What we're seeing now, apart from a whole lot of American flags and 'God Bless Americas,' which were predictable, is this notion that by buying Brand X you're doing your patriotic duty to keep the economy moving." The comment is cynical but true, raising an important question: so what?

Marketers continually strive, in promoting value, quality, price, and image, to convey to their target markets that people who buy and use their products and services or support their issues will feel better for doing so. Making people feel good about a product, service, or issue is a pivotal consideration in a marketing strategy. Cause marketing seeks to take the process even further when the marketer for a company (1) identifies a cause that the company can embrace and believe in, and (2) makes a connection with the constituent group that shares the company's dedication to that cause.

Should patriotism be regarded as a less worthy cause than, say, the environment? Should a passionate desire to help victims of a tragedy as well as their families and their community be less worthwhile than promoting literacy? The short answer, of course, is no. Helping people and communities—the people who support business—is the essence of good business sense, good corporate citizenship, and, simply, good marketing. But what *Advertising Age's* Garfield and others in marketing take exception to is the blatant manipulation of sentiment for profit to a degree that other more sincere efforts (patriotic and otherwise) will be suspect.

Much has been offered here about exercising great care to make certain the company and the cause are a good and sensible fit in a potential partnership. The public should not feel a need to question or challenge the integrity or sincerity of either the company or the cause.

In addition, a serious cause marketing effort should have both uniqueness and substance. A company displaying a flag on its building (or above its logo in ads) or playing *God Bless America* over loudspeakers in its parking lot has not significantly identified itself in a valid way with patriotism or good citizenship. Such strategies used to fall in the category of "mom and apple pie issues"—who would ever line up against them? As marketing strategies, however, displaying flags and playing patriotic songs lack creativity, fail to make unique selling points, and are arguably not an effective allocation of the marketing budget.

As the terrorists' attacks of September 11 become part of history and recede from public consciousness, what will the businesses that sought to identify themselves with the mood of that day do? How solid will their commitment to community be? Speculation among professional marketers is that their efforts in the aftermath of the tragedy will have as much of a lasting effect as those of the dozens of dot-com advertisers that bought million-dollar, half-minute commercial spots on the Super Bowl telecast, only to be forgotten by the time the game ended.

For well-known companies, the stakes are higher. Some people say the companies should know better. "These are times that test the intelligence and sophistication of the marketing person," Clarke Caywood, professor of integrated marketing communications at Northwestern University, told the *Chicago Tribune*. "Anybody who dares to communicate at this time has to understand the risk. They can't be blatantly promotional or exploitive. Some of them are walking the line." Indeed.

Marriott International is known throughout the world for operating fine hotels and resorts. One Marriott hotel, sadly, was located across the street from New York's World Trade Center and was part of the disaster area that came to be known as "ground zero." About two weeks after the terrorist attacks, J. W. Marriott, Jr., the company's chairman and CEO, sent e-mails to customers in the hotel's database expressing "the deepest sorrow and concern" for those "impacted by the tragic events of September 11."

The letter continued, "Many of you, guests and friends with whom we've shared long-standing relationships, have called to check in on us here at Marriott. Your concern is heartwarming and very appreciated." Further, "Through our leave-sharing program, Marriott employees from around the world have donated more than $3 million in leave time to assist their co-workers. The J. Willard and Alice S. Marriott Foundation has also given $1 million to the Marriott Associate Assistance Fund."

Marriott went on to report that his company was "working hard with President Bush and the travel industry to help get America moving again," adding that the company was "offering Marriott's Rewarding Weekends and bonus miles at Renaissance Hotels and Suites. In addition, more than 1,500 Marriott hotels have just re-launched their fall Come Out and Play Weekend rates."

Well. That should certainly take people's minds off the "deep sorrow and concern" mentioned in the letter's opening paragraph. It would seem that when Professor Caywood was warning of the risks of being "blatantly promotional and exploitive," letters like this one were on his mind. And did the chairman perhaps strain credibility just a bit by suggesting past customers of his hotels might have rung the corporate headquarters in Utah after a disaster in New York City to ask how everyone was doing?

Advertising Age and the *Chicago Tribune* noted what has been described as "patriotic grandstanding" in advertising by many of both the largest and smallest companies. *Tribune* media critic Steve Johnson cited, as an example, the ad for Alamo car rentals "that pulled phrases from the Declaration of Independence and *America the Beautiful* to push new, lower rates."

Was this display of patriotic zeal, noticeably absent from advertising and marketing campaigns for several decades, a reflection of a return to genuine patriotism? Or was it marketing at its worst, seizing the moment to engage in a thinly disguised display of shameless opportunism that could undermine sincere cause marketing efforts and render a battle-scarred public even more cynical about advertising, marketing, and the media? The answer to those questions will have to be determined on a case-by-case basis.

No doubt there are truly sincere and honest people who are motivated by a good heart and a dedication to country. No doubt others are somewhat less sincere but are giving the public what they perceive it wants at such times: a reason to come together around a symbol and to believe in something more important than any one of us.

Then there is a third group, the individuals and companies that will commemorate any occasion with a concert, a video, a CD, DVD, a sign, a T-shirt, cap, book, or toy. The occasion can be a visit by the pope, Tall Ships, the celebration of Earth Day, Y2K, the Bicentennial, awareness of world hunger . . . or a terrorist attack. A great number of people perceive the media (and marketers as their partners in crime) to be monsters that need to be fed, and it matters little what the menu lists as the special of the day.

In the wake of such cynicism—and September 11—a desire remains by much of the public to be reassured that there is good in the system and integrity, quality, and value in the businesses that keep the system going.

Marketing is the driving force in the business process, guiding the packaging, positioning, pricing, promotion, and selling of products and services, issues and causes, regardless of the climate of the day.

Marketers understand market cycles. The unique situation that existed with regard to the sagging business environment and the uncertainty that followed September 11 is that, in this instance, the public understood the market forces, is likely to show greater understanding of market forces in the future, and appears to want to be a part of making the marketplace, the economy, and the world better.

The public looks to marketers to provide a reason why it should go to the theater, buy a car, plan a vacation, support a cause. The challenge is to get the message right and communicate it creatively. That has always been the challenge. In a recession or a time of crisis, the urgency is greater but so are the rewards.

It's not easy to sell something to someone who is out of work or can't stop thinking about innocent lives lost so tragically and the fear that comes from knowing it could happen again. Yet that is the challenge confronting marketing people. The response must be a well-crafted, creatively presented, positive message reinforcing expectations of a better tomorrow. Whether the subject is a product or a cause, historically the marketplace has responded better to optimism than to pessimism.

For more than a century, marketing people have painted a very exciting picture and asked that people see themselves in it. The events of September 11, 2001, took a good deal of light and focus from that picture.

Many funds have been created to benefit the families who became victims of the tragedy; other funds focused on rebuilding the damaged New York financial center. Still others were to help police, firefighters, and rescue workers.

The phrase *donor fatigue* has been used to describe the proliferation of well-intentioned efforts, an acknowledgment that there is a limit to how much people can give, whether in cash, time, pledges, or support. A result of the aggressive activity following September 11 is that other good and worthy causes have been cut back or cut off.

The *New York Times* reported: "After an extraordinary string of fat years and rapid growth, the nation's charities are facing the toughest times and the toughest choices in decades . . . These are groups whose revenues have fallen drastically . . . . Across the country, arts groups and some social service organizations are having difficulties. And many of the thousands of new charities formed during the boom, especially those that relied on stock gifts from the newly rich, may not be able to survive."

Some organizations continue to do very well, but many other good causes are at the crossroads. Although no less a challenge, this situation can present meaningful opportunities for companies prepared to undertake a cause marketing effort. Some needs have never been greater and some causes have never been better positioned to form partnerships with companies that have become more sensitized to social responsibility and human needs. Under these circumstances, marketers can be part of the solution in the aftermath of major crises.

One consideration in crisis management is the development of a strategic plan for getting the company or cause back on track, positioned for a future beyond the crisis, beyond the rebuilding period. The same rules apply as in noncrisis situations: be creative, be innovative, and be out front. Don't wait for opportunities. Offer ideas, offer value, and offer benefits.

While waiting for the next "Big Idea," revisit a few programs and ideas that worked in earlier times, and rework them as necessary to meet the demands of the current market environment. Sometimes the most familiar messages resonate as reassuring and effective.

Unfortunately perhaps, even patriotism, when used as a marketing device, goes in cycles and has its limitations. The thought of yet another ad or promotion constructed around a flag takes on a clichéd look subject to charges of gratuitous opportunism (and such observations as that are subject in turn to invectives suggesting the comment is *un*patriotic). In any case, creative renderings that resemble other creative renderings become less effective if they were effective at all. Positioning a company or a cause creatively, with an emphasis on benefits, is a more reliable strategy. The considerations that were inherent in the country's ability to gather strength and become a great world power are the same considerations that, on a relative scale, drive successful businesses: a sense of social responsibility, ethics, integrity, quality, service, and value.

About four months after September 11, the events, concerts, testimonials, and full-page newspaper tributes had subsided. The concert CD to raise funds for New York was relocated to a display away from the front door, and the public's focus shifted back to a sagging economy with an edge of cynicism. The spirit of unity gradually edged back to competitive attack ads in which people and brands tried to advance their own position, not by listing their good qualities, but by trashing the competition. Critics regained their voices and began to question how the tens of millions of dollars collected for families, relief, and rebuilding were being allocated.

The head of the American Red Cross stepped down under fire amid charges that she had allocated funds for purposes other than those the donors had intended. People argued for weeks about why she had done this, suggesting it was likely not an issue of misappropriations but rather one of misunderstanding. Such a misunderstanding, however, can inflict severe and lasting damage on the concept of supporting causes and can undermine public confidence, raising uneasiness among sponsors, contributors, and supporters of other causes as well as of the cause under scrutiny.

Marketers need to carefully examine plans and presentations, addressing and eliminating areas of possible misunderstanding before any program or campaign is launched. A company or organization that commits to a cause in which it truly believes can create a bond with others who believe in and support that cause. Everybody wins. But the company or organization that tries to move with a wave of emotion—to simply take advantage of a moment when people are at their most vulnerable—risks having its efforts backfire and its reputation badly tarnished for a transparent attempt at shameless opportunism.

Business crises (or events with major impact like the tragedy of September 11th) can't be anticipated. But to build a reputation that positions the company or cause as a socially responsible, ethical, accessible public entity permits a greater range of options at a considerably lower cost should circumstances require. What lessons might marketers have learned from how business and the public responded to the events of September 11 and what followed in the immediate months? Listed below are a few.

Avoid inappropriate responses. A response to a major tragic event that is clearly beyond a typical crisis should not be a knee-jerk reaction. The stakes are high. Just as the public is likely to remember the event, it is likely to remember how particular companies and

individuals distinguished themselves—for good or ill—in the aftermath of the event. For this reason, if for no other, a strategy session
is in order to plan an appropriate response or decide if there
should be any response at all.

At that point, the essential elements of the marketing plan (*situation analysis, objectives, strategy and tactics, timeline,* and *budget*)
should be reviewed. By addressing the crisis in this focused way,
determine if a response is in order and, if so, what type of response
would be appropriate. Consider whether your market and stakeholders support your plan or view it as negatively opportunistic.

Live up to expectations. Do what you perceive is expected of
you—or perhaps even more—in the context of your position, market
and industry. Consider some of the following actions that serve as
models of good behavior. McDonald's provided free food to rescue
workers and those in need (but didn't announce it) plus donating $1
million from the McDonald's Corporate checkbook for the relief
effort and an additional $1 million from Ronald McDonald House
Charities. Starbucks donated 750,000 cups of coffee plus $1 million
in corporate cash and a second $1 million in raised contributions.
Microsoft, General Electric, and Daimler Chrysler each pledged
$10 million for disaster relief shortly after the tragedy occurred—
and thereby set the bar against which other large corporations
might be measured. When Kmart distributed millions of paper
American flags, the public, employees, and investors looked to see
what Sears and Wal-Mart would do, for helping in time of need becomes a competitive positioning issue within certain industries.

Create tasteful, not self-serving ads. By placing ads in the national
editions of the *New York Times* and other newspapers to extend sympathy to families of victims and the city itself, as well as to show
support for America (at an open-rate cost of more than $100,000
per page), companies may be criticized by those who have sug-

gested the funds would have been put to better use as cash contributions to the relief efforts or victims' families themselves.

The companies were in fact engaging in an exercise in image
marketing—speaking through their ads to investors, investment
bankers, brokers, regulators, customers, and the public. The ads
were paid representations to position the advertiser as "a classy
company." Such ads, if dignified and understated, can effectively
make their point; if overdone or transparently self-serving, the ads
can backfire.

Corporate ads should serve a greater purpose than pure self-con-
gratulations. Those that required the public to physically appear at
the advertiser's place of business and/or make a purchase to trigger
a contribution are questionable and risky.

Encourage employees to volunteer. Some of the most effective
examples of corporate social responsibility were company employees who volunteered and were observed at the scene by the media
(which took note) giving blood and putting in service time, even
though the companies did not advertise their presence or issue
press releases. On the other hand, companies that promoted their
involvement appeared to be doing it, at least in part, for the publicity and the "credit," which diminished both the sincerity and the
legitimacy of their participation.

The most powerful cause marketing efforts are those that are
well placed and well timed so as to get noticed. Companies that
spend millions to promote their participation are viewed by the
media and more sophisticated members of the public as merely out
for the photo opportunity. Less is more; subtlety works.

Don't promote your good deeds with unsolicited e-mails. E-mails
calling attention to your good deeds lack subtlety and add insult to
injury by suggesting the sender wanted to promote involvement
and get credit, without spending money to do so. It suggests a bit
of the worst of two questionable practices. Members of the public

and businesses that disparage unsolicited e-mails as electronic junk mail, or spam, regard their senders with even lower esteem if the content is largely or exclusively self-serving and wrapped in a bogus purpose.

S U M M A R Y

- From tragedies comes the opportunity to position a company or cause as worthy of public support and respect.

- Patriotic bravado, particularly from businesses and entities that have historically chosen to keep a low public profile, can backfire and be regarded as opportunism and publicity seeking.

- Tying a good act to a worthy cause as conditional—that is, requiring someone to buy your product or service to trigger a contribution—cancels any suggestion of true commitment to the cause.

- Publicists and public relations specialists understand the subtlety of managing to get recognition for good works without advertising it.

- Ads that do take credit for deeds done should at the very least be framed to give credit and thanks to others and have a larger purpose than self-congratulation.

- Companies should be positioned as socially responsible before they need to exploit it.

6

The Cause Marketing Casebook

Some companies are recognized as much for their commitment to—and work on behalf of—particular causes as they are for the products that carry their name. Books have been written about them and their stories are familiar, but those are not the companies chosen as examples in this book. Most of the case studies in this section are from material provided by Business for Social Responsibility (BSR), which has a unique understanding of cause-related marketing and other aspects of socially responsible corporate conduct and positioning. Case studies of ConAgra Foods, Eddie Bauer, Liz Claiborne, Taco Bell, Target, Timberland, Ford Motor Company, Grabber Performance Group, Compaq, Mattel, and Wal-Mart are drawn from BSR's painstaking research, which has not previously been made available to marketers or the public.

Some of the examples are companies well known around the world, whereas others are better known regionally. It is important, however, that the companies and organizations directing cause marketing efforts make certain their programs are known at all—to constituent groups with particular interest in a specific subject as well as to the public in general. Too often, it is assumed that supporters of a cause, customers of a company, and/or the media will notice a cause marketing program, particularly if it is well managed or is for a good cause or simply because it is there. Wrong.

Advertising, public relations, direct marketing, billboards, and sound trucks exist because so much would go unnoticed without them. Marketers, of course, know this. Yet many well-constructed plans are simply folded into an existing marketing program and noted as a footnote or afterthought in a campaign. Given the significant potential of cause marketing programs to increase awareness, shape public opinion, and build loyal supporters, the program deserves better.

As noted in its simplest terms, cause marketing involves a company engaging in an effort to do something for the benefit of the community or a particular constituency, with the hope there will be some payback—that the effort will ultimately benefit the company. Under the best of circumstances, the company is sincere in its aim to do good and actually believes in the cause to which it commits its name and support. In some instances, companies have mounted what were, by most perceptions, merely public relations campaigns conceived for the purpose of enhancing a corporate image, pumping up a stock price, or getting those pesky regulators off the corporate back.

There have been times when it didn't matter. The public was willing to accept a company's doing the right thing for the wrong reason. At least someone would benefit, and in the end that was what was important. That, however, is not how it works anymore. People pay attention, form opinions, and in some instances respond dramatically.

WHERE THERE'S SMOKE . . .

The public in the 21st century has grown more sophisticated in how it processes and evaluates the information it receives. For example, all through the 1950s and early 1960s, tobacco companies donated gift cartons of their cigarettes to members of the U.S. military, despite the fact that schools at the time were teaching, and parents were telling their children, that cigarette smoking was "bad

for you." The tobacco companies not only kept giving away free cigarettes, but they cheerfully continued to advertise their generosity,
believing that it amounted to good publicity for the companies and
their brands.

Times change, but, alas, the ability of some corporations to read
public sentiment apparently doesn't. Decades later, smoking was
classified as a health hazard in a class by itself, with special legislation governing warning labels, advertising restrictions, and age
requirements for purchasing tobacco products.

Philip Morris

By the year 2000, Philip Morris, arguably the largest of the tobacco giants, was roundly criticized for running a hugely expensive
advertising campaign that sought to make public its many good
deeds—deeds that apparently consisted mainly of writing checks to
respected organizations like Meals-on-Wheels and the Thurgood
Marshall Scholarship Fund. Full-page color ads appeared with frequency in high-circulation magazines, such as *People* and *Time*. A TV
version of the ad campaign ran during Sunday morning news
shows, a media buy aimed not so much at the general public as at
affluent and influential individuals, legislators, and government
agency regulators. The campaign that cost millions of dollars was
not only ineffective by virtually any measure but was openly derided
by many marketing professionals and much of the public, according
to published reports. The derision was not just a dismissive wave
from the usual antitobacco activist groups: it was derision by virtually everyone.

That a Philip Morris spokesperson would tell the *Wall Street Journal* the company believed it was "viewed as changing for the better
and being more socially responsible" is a pathetic example of a
company out of touch with public sentiment, refusing to see what
everyone else seemed to: a totally transparent attempt to portray a

giant tobacco company as good guys who were perhaps just misunderstood. Uh-huh.

Such a position, from a marketing standpoint, undermines the company to a point where whatever it says or does becomes suspect. This is not a very good position for a company and an industry already on the defensive with much of the public and many legislators.

Earlier, this same company had sponsored a heavily advertised, five-state touring exhibition of the National Archives celebration of the 200th anniversary of the Bill of Rights. Philip Morris's promotional materials described the presentation to the public as "an extraordinary exhibition that will capture their eyes, their ears and, most of all, their hearts. They'll be enveloped by history, transported into the present, and reenter the world with a new appreciation of our freedoms."

The sentiment might have been more moving if the company had not made it abundantly clear that it was really concerned with one freedom in particular—the freedom of its major constituents. These were cigarette smokers who were being told by restaurants, the public, and commercial building managers across the United States to "take it outside."

In this instance as well, the company's true motives were transparent, its emphasis misplaced in the face of overwhelming public sentiment. Its hidden agenda, however, was not very well hidden. Philip Morris was not only on the wrong side of an issue but its defense was indirect and convoluted; because it seemed to realize its cause was so unpopular, it undertook a strategy to wrap it within a socially acceptable cause. Smokers kept buying the company's products, but few were buying the logic of its argument.

If Philip Morris's objective was to defend the rights of smokers, that's what it should have done. If, in its recent campaigns, the company wants to be regarded as a generous, socially responsible corporate citizen, there are more creative and less obvious—less deceptive—moves it could make.

One extremely common strategy is to use testimonials. Philip Morris could have the recipients of the company's generosity acknowledge it in press releases, ads, or literature of its own—not material painted with the logos of the various Philip Morris companies. A nonprofit organization, such as Meals-on-Wheels, might have announced its goal for the coming year, noting all the good it had done for people in preceding years and listing the corporate benefactors that made it possible, perhaps even noting the size of the companies' contributions. This strategy would have (1) appeared not so self-serving on Philip Morris's part; (2) would have listed Philip Morris among several other less controversial corporations, perhaps allowing it to enjoy a "halo effect" from such associations; (3) would have gained the company a bit of uncharacteristic humility; (4) would have, perhaps, shown the company as a consistently good corporate citizen over several years, though it had never chosen to publicize it; and would have (5) allowed the company to respond with a public statement that it was glad it was able to do some good—prompting at least some people to believe the company maybe wasn't all bad and had perhaps been judged too harshly. Sure, it sold cigarettes and that was bad, but at least that wasn't the only thing it did, and it did put some of its profits to good use.

Another approach would have been to run a series of "open letter" ads in which the company listed its financial and other contributions to good causes over the past several years. This approach would be totally self-serving, but it would be open, honest, direct, and encompassing. A headline such as "The Philip Morris Companies—We're More Than You Thought We Were" followed by ad copy that lists millions of dollars in cash and products (not tobacco products but perhaps inventory from its Kraft Foods unit or other divisions) donated to a roster of worthy and needy causes. This strategy would have been more effective than the expensive four-color magazine ads and television commercials that repeated the Philip Morris name five times more often than the name of the organization the company was supposed to be helping.

For decades Mobil Oil Corporation (and later Exxon Mobil) ran "advertorials" in major newspapers, directly explaining—without apology—the company's position on controversial issues involving the oil industry and the public interest. People did not always agree, but the company won respect for not ducking the issues or defensively trying to obscure them.

The public respects directness in advertisers, particularly corporate giants. Philip Morris Companies' attempts at cause marketing through the years appear to be anything but direct. Perhaps that explains why, in a survey reported by the *Wall Street Journal* in January 2002, of 60 companies ranked according to which the public believed are socially responsible, Philip Morris was number 59. The public was not about to give credit where it clearly believed no credit was due.

Marketing can be a useful way of solving a problem, but a company must first acknowledge it has a problem if any solution is to work.

A RECIPE FOR HELP

In the best of situations, a cause will have some relationship to the product or company that works for its benefit. A global conglomerate and leader in the food industry saw a need that fit its purpose, its products, and its corporate conscience.

ConAgra Foods

Business for Social Responsibility (BSR) cites ConAgra Foods' 1999 launch of its Feeding Children Better program as a well-conceived effort that created the largest corporate initiative dedicated solely to ending childhood hunger in the United States.

ConAgra, America's second largest food company and the parent company of more than 80 brands, including Healthy Choice, Butterball, and Orville Redenbacher, entered into a partnership with

America's Second Harvest and other antihunger organizations to create a program that would (1) feed hungry children, (2) bring more food into the charitable food distribution system, and (3) focus greater national attention on the issue of childhood hunger. The company had engaged in considerable philanthropic activity before its management concluded that the company's efforts had become too scattered. It decided that ConAgra could have a greater impact by forging a long-term commitment to a single cause.

Noting that as many as 12 million children each year were affected by hunger in the United States, the company chose to make hunger its cause. Statistics indicated that one in three mothers leaving welfare did not know where to find her child's next meal. Capitalizing on its food industry connection and expertise, the Feeding Children Better program was designed to leverage ConAgra's extensive food sales and distribution network at the same time it met its philanthropic commitment to its designated cause. Using the special skills and talents of a marketing and public relations firm that specialized in cause marketing, ConAgra established clear objectives for the program.

The company approached America's Second Harvest because that organization had a distinguished history and a deep commitment to the problem of hunger. As the largest hunger relief organization in the United States, America's Second Harvest had built a network of more than 200 regional food banks and food rescue organizations serving all 50 states.

The ConAgra Feeding Children Better Foundation was created to manage the formal partnership. Agreements were made between ConAgra, America's Second Harvest, and the Center on Hunger and Poverty. The group became the Center on Hunger, Poverty and Nutrition Policy at Tufts University; its mission is to promote policies that improve the lives and developmental capacities of low-income children and families in the United States. The agreements define the program's goals, objectives, and the responsibilities of each partner. The foundation's president had the primary responsibility for coordinating the program's activities with corporate and business unit communications, marketing, and executive management teams, while the communications director of America's Second Harvest coordinated the nonprofit's activities.

Though most of the financial contributions ConAgra made were through the foundation, public awareness campaigns and cause marketing promotions were financed through the various marketing budgets of the ConAgra food companies. In this way, it was not only the parent company but the various brands that were able to establish a connection to the Feeding Children Better program.

In contrast with other companies that simply write checks to worthy causes in the name of philanthropy and good corporate citizenship, ConAgra's contributions to its cause (and its cause marketing program) are real. For example, by providing funding to update computer software tracking and additional trucking, the program increased the speed with which food moved through the food bank network and reclaimed millions of pounds of food that would have otherwise gone to waste. ConAgra's Rapid Food Distribution system greatly simplified the ways in which America's Second Harvest procures and distributes charitable food donations.

The company also committed itself to purchasing delivery trucks for almost half of the network's 200 food banks as well as funding 100 new Kids Cafes—the "for kids only" after-school programs that provide free nutritious meals to children in safe community-based nonprofit programs such as the Boys and Girls Clubs.

Generating public awareness of the program and educating the public about its aims and its importance are critical. A star-studded event launched the Feeding Children Better program during National Food Bank Week in 1999. The event and its timing attracted considerable media attention as well as the interest of political leaders and others of influence, particularly those associated with the cause of world hunger relief.

ConAgra was represented at a high-profile press event with the Center on Hunger and Poverty, Senator Edward Kennedy, and leading hunger relief advocates, at which time the most comprehensive analysis on hunger in the United States in several years was released.

The company also secured the support of the Ad Council, which committed itself to a three-year, multimedia public awareness campaign with an estimated $28 million a year in donated print and broadcast media. In addition, the Web sites of ConAgra Foods and America's Second Harvest offered information about the campaign, and a unique Feeding Children Better Web site and toll-free telephone number were created as part of the Ad Council's campaign. It was estimated that Feeding Children Better garnered more than 86 million media impressions between 1999 and 2001.

In addition to its cash contributions, ConAgra Foods donated more than 200 tons of its food products to launch the campaign program—enough to provide 300,000 meals. The company subsequently donated additional millions of pounds of food to food banks in the name of Feeding Children Better.

The company's various business units also became actively involved in the program. One of ConAgra's brands, County Line Deli Cheese, developed a cause marketing promotion in grocery stores across the United States to benefit Feeding Children Better. After the brand pledged to donate a portion of its revenue to the cause, its sales volume exceeded expectations by 16 percent. The resulting donation provided enough funds to finance the opening of five new ConAgra Feeding Children Better Kids Cafes. County Line's announcement that it intended to continue the promotion resulted in more good publicity for the brand and more goodwill.

ConAgra employees took an active part in the program as well. In 1999 and 2000 the company's CEO issued a holiday challenge, which prompted employees to donate over 200,000 pounds of food. More than 70 of the company's plants and operating facilities responded in the food drives, through which ConAgra offered grants to winning communities of employees for local feeding programs. This afforded opportunities to again extend awareness of the program and generate goodwill among both ConAgra employees and the various communities. The challenges that called on employees to take an active role in the program for the benefit of their communities were considered so successful that the company made them an annual event each holiday season.

A ConAgra Feeding Children Better Cafe was also selected to create holiday cards that would be offered for sale to ConAgra Foods employees, providing yet another opportunity for the company's own people to support the program and feel a greater sense of personal participation. Proceeds from the sale of the cards went to the ConAgra Feeding Children Better Foundation.

As BSR's cause-related marketing partnership guidelines note, cause marketing programs function best when the partnership of company and nonprofit organization has shared, yet specific, goals, benefits, and responsibilities and is very clear about each one. In the case of ConAgra Foods and America's Second Harvest, the shared goals are to get the food to children who need it, raise awareness of the problem of childhood hunger, and repair breakdowns in the charitable food distribution system.

ConAgra's specific goals were to demonstrate its commitment to social responsibility as a core corporate value, have a deep and long-lasting impact on a cause, provide opportunities to deepen its relationship with both key retail and food service customers, become a rallying point for its more than 80,000 employees and ten business units, and honor its customers and employees by helping to improve the communities in which they live and work.

The goals of America's Second Harvest were to raise new funds to support and expand its campaign and programs on a national level, and to build institutional credibility through a long-term, substantive partnership with a respected national company.

ConAgra Foods made an initial three-year commitment to the program at a cost of $11.5 million, plus additional millions of dollars in product donations. The company's impact on the cause has had measurable results. It has financed 47 Kids Cafes, each of which serves an average of 12,000 meals per year (and when all scheduled

Kids Cafes are opened, it is expected some 1 million meals per year will be served to children). The company's Rapid Food Distribution System helped America's Second Harvest distribute more than 36 million pounds of fresh produce (a 104 percent increase over the previous year) and 1.4 million pounds of frozen fish (a 40 percent increase) to food banks across the United States during 2000 alone. As this information was being compiled, 29 new trucks had been purchased with grants from ConAgra Foods; and the company's business units have developed deeper and stronger relationships with their local communities and food banks.

For its part, ConAgra has noted a significant impact on the company. In 1999, Feeding Children Better was named Campaign of the Year and Community Relations Campaign of the Year by *PR Week* magazine, and it received an award as well from *Inside PR* magazine for the Best Corporate Philanthropy Program.

The company believes it has also seen signs of improved relations with its employees, business units, industry, and customers for having created a program that presents the company as a good and socially responsible corporate citizen. Each of these groups has acknowledged its pride—and ConAgra's reputation has been enhanced—in putting childhood hunger in the spotlight and raising awareness of this important issue across the United States. By any measure, this is an example of a case where it seems that through commitment, planning, and action, everybody wins.

KEEPING THE GREAT OUTDOORS GREAT

In the current media climate, reporters are often looking for instances where companies can be tripped up and held accountable when their public and private faces bear little resemblance. Some companies dedicate themselves to keeping a low profile and trying to dodge the bullet. Others thoughtfully craft a plan to make a difference and stand for the concerns they know are important to their public.

Eddie Bauer

Mention Eddie Bauer to most members of the general public and the response is likely to relate to the Great Outdoors. The apparel retailer has, after all, spent decades cultivating its corporate image as a store for environmentalists and outdoor enthusiasts. It was not surprising then that when the company chose to undertake a long-term cause marketing effort, its cause would somehow be environmentally connected.

Although Eddie Bauer had been involved in several projects over the years, the company had no national environmental program before 1995. This would not have been an issue for most other businesses, but for Eddie Bauer, with its close association to outdoor life and activities, the point did seem to represent a serious omission. What made matters a bit more dicey was the fact that a significant portion of the company's business came from catalog sales, and in the early 1990s it found itself under attack by activists who criticized the quantity of paper used to produce the catalogs—even though only tree-farmed wood products were used.

In response to these concerns and to show its determination to commit to a serious national environmental program, Eddie Bauer began its search for the right partner to help it follow through on this commitment. After carefully researching a number of environmental organizations, the company narrowed its focus to American Forests as a potential partner.

American Forests is the oldest nonprofit conservation organization in the United States and is a world leader in tree planting for environmental restoration. Based on the organization's distinguished history and its excellent reputation among consumers—environmentalists in particular—Eddie Bauer believed a cause marketing partnership would serve both parties well.

American Forests had already begun developing nontraditional funding sources years earlier and had also engaged in several successful corporate partnerships. It saw Eddie Bauer's environmental positioning and products as a complement to its own image and position. The two sides began discussions in 1994 and in October 1995 established a formal partnership. Together they created the Eddie Bauer Global ReLeaf Tree Project.

Eddie Bauer is the largest single corporate contributor to the Global ReLeaf campaign, and the effort is the company's primary cause-related marketing program. In 2000 it expanded its commitment to American Forests reforestation efforts with the creation of Wildfire ReLeaf. This reforestation and education program responds directly to the devastation of American forest ecosystems caused by forest fires. Recognizing the specific reforestation needs that result from the significant number of forest fires occurring each year in the United States, the partnership has been extended to focus solely on the issue of Wildfire ReLeaf.

Even though Eddie Bauer had originally organized the program through its marketing department, with the assistance and involvement of its community affairs staff, the structure shifted over time and would later be coordinated by the company's corporate social responsibility department (community relations, public affairs, and government affairs) with support from a cross-functional team that included members of the marketing, accounting, and public relations departments.

For its part, American Forests had a person on staff who was responsible for managing its corporate relationships. The considerable attention Eddie Bauer showed the program, utilizing the expertise of its various corporate professionals from different areas of business, underscores the importance the company attached to the program. To support its administration of the effort—including public relations, membership, development, and tree-planting managers—the organization deducts a percentage fee from donations it receives. The Eddie Bauer Global ReLeaf Tree Project introduced the "Add a Dollar, Plant a Tree" program, which invites the retailer's customers to participate by adding a contribution to their catalog, online, and in-store purchases, with proceeds going to the fund.

Inside the company, employees began an associate pledge drive through which they could directly contribute to the tree-planting fund through payroll deductions. On the executive level, the CEO and president actively promoted the program through public appearances, and other members of senior management lent their expertise in marketing, advertising, and strategic planning.

Eddie Bauer employees also serve as volunteers, helping to plant trees at locations across the United States. The company has given American Forests seedling gift packs and memberships to business associates and clients as well as enlisting a credit card company in a special month-long promotion. In that arrangement, 30¢ from each Eddie Bauer purchase made using the credit card was donated to the fund until the donations reached $50,000.

From its own corporate contributions budget, Eddie Bauer provides an annual unrestricted grant to American Forests. To date, as this report is compiled, the total amount of such grants exceeds $250,000.

The cause marketing partnership arranges and promotes planting and other events for regional reforestation campaigns. In 1999 Eddie Bauer sponsored an American Forests Conference, at which it announced the company had met its goal of planting 2.5 million trees. That same year, to celebrate the 100th birthday of the company's founder and namesake, Eddie Bauer donated 500,000 live tree seedlings to American Forests for planting.

Other promotions included issuing a special CD for sale, with one dollar from each sale going to the Eddie Bauer Global ReLeaf Fund; introducing an annual holiday sale featuring seedling gift packs at Eddie Bauer stores; and a reception in Washington, D.C., on Capitol Hill to launch the Wildfire ReLeaf program in 2001 as well as to celebrate the 125th anniversary of American Forests.

As a cause marketing program, the effort has been promoted visually and at every possible location and opportunity. In-store signage, brochures, print ads, and information in the Eddie Bauer catalog and on the company Web site provide continuing visibility.

An associate reeducation effort helped to communicate program goals and development through payroll stuffers and other internal materials. A company-sponsored insert on American Forests was included in a special issue of *Business Week,* while ads and updates in *American Forests* magazine help support the program's message.

The partnership had hoped to plant 5 million trees and raise $5 million over a seven-year period for the Global ReLeaf program. Wildfire ReLeaf's goal was to have planted 1 million trees by 2002.

On the corporate side, Eddie Bauer wanted to strengthen its brand image as a company concerned about environmental matters in addition to enhancing the level of its customer and employee loyalty particularly in and around the company's Pacific Northwest headquarters.

At the same time, American Forests defined its mission as helping people improve the environment with trees and forests. Its hope is to provide Eddie Bauer customers and employees with tangible and relevant opportunities to contribute to a better environment.

Eddie Bauer, through its cause marketing program, is furthering its identification with environmental concerns. By contributing cash and coordinating a wide and active program of volunteerism and promotional activities involving its managers and employees on a continuing basis, the company will likely advance and maintain its reputation as a leading conservation-oriented corporate citizen.

By mid-1999, more than 2 million trees (representing more than $2 million) had been planted through the Eddie Bauer Global ReLeaf Project, reforesting more than 50 sites in North America. By the end of 2000, some 3 million trees had been planted, exceeding the original goal by 500,000. In one year of the program alone, Eddie Bauer employees raised more than $70,000 from employee contributions, a strong indication of support by the company's own people.

The Eddie Bauer-American Forests partnership has also been honored by the National Resource Council of America with an Award for Achievement in Development. The cause marketing effort has raised awareness of environmental issues and of the marketer's role as well. In terms of benefits to the company, Eddie Bauer is no longer on the defensive when questions of its environmental commitment arise. It has examined its own environmental practices and established recycling initiatives in its operations. A 1998 informal survey provided by BSR found that 90 percent of Eddie Bauer customers in the Northwest were aware of the cause marketing program and that recognition among repeat customers was particularly high.

MARKETING TO WOMEN

Each year new research underscores the importance of women to marketers as studies show women taking on greater responsibility and increasingly assuming the role of decision makers, not only in traditional situations as homemakers, but as managers of small businesses, large companies, entrepreneurships, car pools, and the family budget. Women, more than men, choose cold remedies and brands of soap, and are also more knowledgeable in the comparative quality of big ticket items, from cars to insurance policies, home security systems, and travel.

As a demographic target, women continue to represent the market for the long-successful glamour magazines that include such titles as *Vanity Fair* and *Harpers Bazaar* and new or refashioned publications like Oprah Winfrey's *O* and Rosie O'Donnell's *Rosie*. What were once women's pages are now recast as lifestyle pages of newspapers, though they are still largely aimed at women. And women are also the target audience for many of the features in business and general interest media, a category largely aimed at men exclusively in the past.

Within the demographic wheel, marketers recognize the power of women in a broad range of categories (college-educated working mothers, single working mothers as heads of households, stay-at-home moms, soccer moms, managers of home-based businesses, community service volunteers, professional women, women who advise presidents, etc.). The modern marketplace is rich with an abundance of women's issues that represent a range of opportunities unimagined not so long ago. A company considering a cause marketing program in such an environment will find myriad possibilities and certainly no shortage of good and worthy causes.

But like companies that break from the pack to become great success stories within and outside the mainstream, an effective cause marketing program aimed at women should offer something no other program offers.

Obviously, the aim of all marketing programs is to be different or unique, though at times that doesn't seem possible. That is why most marketing departments have someone with the title of creative director. Despite the fact that some marketers try to reduce any subject to "the product" as if they were selling soap and insist that it's all the same regardless of the subject, it's not the same. Products and services are and can be different. A cause or an issue very often won't have the same attributes as a product or brand and will not easily lend itself to formulaic marketing methods.

Certainly the principles of effective marketing can be applied to a subject, but when one considers the causes of literacy, animal rights, gun control, adoption, clean air, AIDS—no, it's not the same as selling soap. An important distinction of a cause is its inherent element of uniqueness or importance that is in some way emotionally or psychologically meaningful to a particular constituency. The many causes that can be termed *women's issues* reflect that philosophy.

Liz Claiborne

Business for Social Responsibility cites as worthy of note the campaign Women's Work, a public awareness and cause-related marketing program launched in 1991 by Liz Claiborne, designer and marketer of women's apparel, fragrances, and accessories. In

1993, the company decided that it could maximize its resources by focusing exclusively on the issue of domestic violence. Building a high-profile campaign around an issue whose importance no one will challenge but is nonetheless one that many find too disturbing to discuss was an extraordinary decision.

Liz Claiborne entered into relationships with a number of local and national nonprofit organizations for different aspects of the program but chose as its primary partner the Family Violence Prevention Fund. Clearly, for a style-conscious company in Liz Claiborne's position, its choice of a cause is not one likely to soon be on the fashion pages.

According to BSR, Liz Claiborne surveyed women, including its customers, about issues of most importance to them and learned that domestic violence was a top concern. Subsequently, the company addressed the subject in one of its Women's Work pilot programs that was presented in San Francisco. It then commissioned local artists to create a series of images of domestic violence. The company also provided funding for what became the first centralized 24-hour domestic violence hot line in the San Francisco area.

Quickly absorbing the lessons of this experience, Liz Claiborne decided to make domestic violence its sole focus as a cause, noting this was an area greatly underserved and believing it could make an impact.

It was during the San Francisco program that Liz Claiborne came into contact with the Family Violence Prevention Fund, which asked for the company's help in bringing its message to a national audience. The company assisted the fund at first by enlisting its advertising agency, which agreed to work pro bono for the fund's campaign.

Liz Claiborne also introduced people from the fund to the Ad Council, which agreed to produce a national public service announcement on domestic violence that was eventually distributed to some 22,000 media outlets across the United States. In turn, Liz Claiborne asked the fund to provide its expertise in helping to develop the company's program on domestic violence awareness, education, and prevention.

The two entities agreed to work together under an informal partnership arrangement for special projects. The company's communications department managed the relationship, with assistance from various members of senior management and departments of the company on an as-needed basis—including Liz Claiborne's chairman.

The company's outside marketing firm, PT & Co., plays a major role in developing and implementing the Women's Work program. The firm, in fact, became so much involved in the domestic violence program that the relationship came to be regarded as a three-way partnership, in which the Family Violence Prevention Fund, Liz Claiborne, and the marketing firm functioned as equals.

In mounting its cause marketing program, the partners share the goals of raising awareness of domestic violence and of finding solutions to the problem as well. They are committed to educating the public through prevention materials and programs.

Liz Claiborne hopes not only to demonstrate the company's commitment to social responsibility but also to generate goodwill and be responsive to consumer expectations that companies contribute to the communities they serve. Clearly, the company's corporate commitment to addressing domestic violence extends beyond the borders of the world of fashion.

The Family Violence Prevention Fund aims to use the cause marketing program to raise funds to support its work and its community-based domestic violence prevention efforts. In addition, the fund is hoping to build institutional credibility through a long-term partnership with a respected national corporation and expand its programs throughout the United States.

Liz Claiborne provides money to the fund and other nonprofit organizations through an annual holiday card grant program. The company's employees and affiliates take part in the program on a number of levels. Liz Claiborne offers domestic violence awareness and assistance programs to its employees; maintains programs that provide trained counselors; and distributes brochures, memos, posters, and payroll inserts along with maintaining open hot lines.

The company holds an annual Charity Shopping Day on which a percentage of sales from its stores is donated to local domestic violence organizations. Consumers can order domestic violence education and prevention materials through toll-free numbers maintained by the company in collaboration with the fund. Materials can also be downloaded from the company's Web site. A line of Women's Work merchandise, including jewelry, handbags, hats, mugs, and T-shirts, can be ordered through toll-free numbers, with the proceeds donated to the fund.

The company has produced educational materials, such as *What You Need to Know About Dating Violence: A Teen's Handbook* and *A Woman's Handbook: A Practical Guide to Discussing Relationship Abuse,* as well as other materials, programs, and messages for TV, billboards, and other media.

Since the inception of the program, Liz Claiborne has generated tremendous publicity for the Women's Work campaign and is convinced that its cause marketing effort has enhanced its reputation as a socially responsible company. It is a company that knows and understands its market and has chosen to engage its constituents in a cause that falls well outside its usual stylish and glamorous surroundings.

Liz Claiborne does not track the program's effect on its sales, believing it is not possible to measure the impact accurately. It does believe the program has enhanced its reputation as a socially responsible company and reports considerable anecdotal evidence from customers and employees who now more positively associate the Liz Claiborne brand with efforts to raise domestic violence awareness and education. It is a risk the company took, and it appears to have paid off.

FOOD FOR THOUGHT FOR THE FUTURE

Fast food might be fun food to the younger generation that so often determines chains' and franchisers' market share, but when it comes to cause marketing, it is serious business all the way. Today's young customer represents not only a potential adult customer but an opportunity to make the world a better place, one generation at a time.

Taco Bell

BSR points to Taco Bell as an example of a fast-food operation that found the most demographically suited partner to achieve noteworthy success beyond the drive-up window.

The national fast-food franchise established the Taco Bell Foundation in 1992 as a vehicle to raise and donate funds to community causes. Early efforts involved fundraising with customers contributing to marked in-store canisters and proceeds going to the Red Cross and other disaster relief agencies. But in 1994, the foundation committed itself to developing an issue-focused program.

When J.D. Power & Associates surveyed Taco Bell customers and employees, it learned that education, teen violence, crime, and pregnancy prevention were the major concerns of the company's main constituent groups. From the research firm's list of prospective cause marketing partners, Taco Bell decided to approach Boys & Girls Clubs of America because its issues were Taco Bell's customers' issues, and the organization had both national visibility and a fine reputation.

The nonprofit organization was interested in a Taco Bell partnership, which it saw as an opportunity to reach teenagers, a group it had found more difficult to connect with than its typical 6-year-old to 12-year-old members. The clubs offered Taco Bell what it called a plan for "proposal-less fundraising," a method for developing a program that would meet both the company's and the nonprofit organization's goals and increase the likelihood the partnership would succeed.

Boys & Girls Clubs of America's guiding principles for its strategic alliances specify that it (1) has the right to determine which companies it will work with; (2) will not endorse products or maintain an exclusive partnership arrangement with any single company or product; (3) will not guarantee specific returns to a company based on any alliance; and (4) may independently investigate all legal, tax, and public relations issues related to the partner and partnership. Taco Bell and the clubs developed a formal written agreement spelling out each side's objectives, specific fundraising goals, and a time for the partnership arrangement.

Taco Bell's goals were to increase the impact of its foundation's philanthropic giving with a coordinated national awareness program, make a significant impact on a cause that mattered to the company's customers and employees, and raise $15 million for Boys & Girls Clubs of America through in-store canister placements and other fundraising activities.

Boys & Girls Clubs of America wanted to build awareness for its organization and its partners, raise funds for the national organization and to support local club programs, and expand its reach to directly influence a greater percentage of 13-year-olds to 18-year-olds.

The resulting program was dubbed TEENSupreme and would involve the following:

- Creation of TEENSupreme Centers in Boys & Girls Clubs (or at separate locations) with a dedicated staff and space for teen-oriented programming and activity (including an emphasis on career exploration, job preparation, and placement)

- TEENSupreme Keystone Clubs, small, peer-driven clubs where members aged 14 to 18 teach citizenship and leadership through club projects and community service

- TEENSupreme Academy, a training program that teaches club-related skills, including working with teens, recruiting, mentoring, and education

- TEENSupreme Career Prep, programs funded by the U.S. Departments of Labor and Justice providing career counseling, skills training, job placement for Boys & Girls Club members (where appropriate, Taco Bell and its franchises make an effort to place participants in Taco Bell stores)

- CLUBService, a three-way partnership involving Taco Bell, Boys & Girls Clubs of America, and the Corporation for National Service, providing educational grants to 17-year-old and 18-year-old club members who engage in community service in their local club and community.

Clearly, this is an ambitious undertaking and the partners' shared goals for it included:

- Opening 100 TEENSupreme Centers throughout the United States by the end of 2001 to serve more than 65,000 teens

- Training 400 Boys & Girls Club professional staffers annually as mentors through the TEENSupreme Academies, with 2,000 trained teen mentors by the end of 2001

- Expanding the number of TEENSupreme Keystone Clubs to 800 by the end of 2000 to serve more than 12,000 teens who receive leadership development training (this goal was actually exceeded as nearly 1,000 clubs were chartered by the end of 2000)

- Enrolling 1,300 teens in TEENSupreme CLUBService programs by 2001

- Enrolling 5,000 teens in the TEENSupreme Career Prep program and placing 4,000 of these participants in jobs by 2001.

The company solicits its employees and vendors for participation in the program and relies on press releases, press kits, and in-store canisters to tell its story. Perhaps more could be done on the media front to raise awareness, but clearly the program's results—70 TEENSupreme Centers operating throughout the United States serving more than 70,000 teens; 927 Keystone Clubs chartered in 2000 and another 535 in 2001; 1,863 professionals trained; 1,202 teens participating in the service program; and 4,500 teens placed in jobs—are impressive, having exceeded expectations.

Taco Bell found its own cause to reach its own constituency in a positive and ambitious program. It clearly knows and understands its market.

A RETAILER POSITIONS ITSELF BY HELPING A FRIEND IN NEED

Retail department stores offer something for everyone, often resulting in a corporate image in shades of gray. The best a retailer can hope for is to find a space on the spectrum—upscale, low-end, or the rarely exciting midrange. America's long-time top retailer has been struggling to hang on since the 1980s, reinventing itself every few years, buying and adding new companies to its mix, divesting itself of others. Another giant that literally changed the culture of retailing in the last quarter of the 20th century—offering designer labels, celebrity brand names, and deep discounts in shopping carts under a rotating spotlight—filed for bankruptcy protection in 2002. As much of the public turns to specialty stores and the convenience of the Internet, the department store that was a fixture of generations past must find ways to reach out and redefine itself.

So when a retailer decides to become part of a cause marketing effort, we may suspect that, more than many types of companies, it is trying to help itself—to forge an identity and a bond with a constituency that being a large, modern-day general store makes more difficult.

Target Stores

According to BSR, Target Stores, a division of Target Corporation, decided to develop a national cause marketing campaign to coincide with the launch of its in-store pharmacy concept. The company's objective was to establish its commitment to a cause and, at the same time, differentiate its Target pharmacies from competitors.

Target's research found St. Jude Children's Research Hospital in Memphis, Tennessee, a highly desirable cause marketing partner. The facility has an excellent reputation and considerable status as an internationally recognized research facility respected throughout the world. The fact that St. Jude Hospital can register an impact beyond its home community of Memphis is important as is its mission: to treat all patients, regardless of their ability to pay.

Target is a well-regarded chain of stores but is not considered upscale, nor is it identified with prescriptions or pharmaceuticals. It is positioned to appeal to the desire of average-income people for quality and style in general merchandise. St. Jude is an institution that puts people's needs first, regardless of position or income. Both partners seemed to be sending the public a similar message in terms of priorities.

As it prepared to launch its new pharmacies, Target saw the value in a possible partnership with St. Jude as well as an opportunity to identify the stores with a good cause. Target first approached St. Jude Hospital about a possible cause marketing effort in 1996. The original arrangement called for the company to sponsor hospital programs, helping to provide general support and funding. But as the two organizations began working together, Target became aware of St. Jude's lack of long-term affordable housing for patients and their families. The company saw an opportunity to respond to a need, to make a meaningful contribution to a well-regarded nonprofit organization and its clients by helping to develop a tangible, long-term, branded project that Target customers and employees

Target House is a facility for families of seriously ill children who are patients at St. Jude Children's Research Hospital in Memphis. The retailer provides funding and promotional support, as well as an opportunity for its employees and vendors to support the cause on a variety of levels. (Photo of the author at Target House by Karin Gottschalk Marconi)

could relate to. Similar facilities had done a great deal to help position the nation's leading fast-food restaurant chain as a humanitarian organization. A Memphis-based facility under the Target banner would have the unique St. Jude Children's Hospital connection that would help to give it its own identity.

Early on, St. Jude had shared its corporate partnership guidelines with Target. The guidelines addressed a range of issues, such as internal communications policies, the kinds of products to which a promotion could be tied, how a promotion could be conducted, and the minimum donation percentage. Although there was some flexibility in the guidelines, the St. Jude organization insists on explicit written agreements, knowing that such documents greatly reduce the likelihood of misunderstanding and unmet expectations.

It was agreed that Target, through donations and fundraising, would help to establish Target House, a free housing facility for patients and their families receiving long-term care at St. Jude. Target House opened in 1999 with 50 suites in addition to exercise facilities, playrooms, a library, and a music room. In 2001, construction began on Target House 2, added an additional 46 suites and the Scott Hamilton Family Fitness Center, the Scott Hamilton Arts and Crafts Center, and an outdoor pavilion funded by the Tiger Woods Foundation.

The Target-St. Jude Hospital cause marketing partnership is administered by a team that includes representatives from the company's community relations, marketing, merchandising, advertising, and special events departments, who meet as needed to work on various aspects of the program—usually weekly or biweekly as special events and promotions demand. Target staff people travel to Memphis on a regular basis for face-to-face meetings with hospital staff to provide support for events taking place at Target House. The company's community relations corporate giving budget donates money to run the program, with in-store and television advertising funding drawn from the company's advertising budget. The special events and PR departments fund events at Target House.

Initially, Target donated a portion of all sales from its pharmacies, but because not all Target stores have pharmacies—and the company wanted to involve the largest number of stores possible—the promotion was expanded to include a portion of sales on all health-related products. This took the relationship beyond the one intended to help promote Target's pharmacies to a larger cause marketing relationship.

Each quarter the company sends outstanding employee volunteers to tour Target House and St. Jude Hospital and to participate in a carnival for the facility's patients. Several hundred such trips for employees from around the United States have resulted in these employees spreading the word about the program and its value to their fellow employees. Feedback indicates that visits to the site have a positive and lasting impression on Target employees.

Several of the company's vendors of health, beauty, and other products have developed product promotions of their own, with a portion of the proceeds going to Target House and St. Jude Hospital. Other vendors have donated furnishings and supplies for construction and upkeep. And some vendors have participated in a promotion for Target House, whereby certain rooms at the facility will carry the sponsoring company's or individual's name.

Adding a dignified, yet theatrical, touch, Target recruited celebrities to speak and help promote Target House at St. Jude Hospital, all of whom had some connection that made their participation noteworthy: Singing star Amy Grant, a Tennessee native who appears in Target ads; golf superstar Tiger Woods, whose foundation donated the outdoor pavilion to Target House 2; and ice skating star Scott Hamilton (headliner of the "Target Stars on Ice" tour), whose name is on the two dedicated centers that are part of the Target House program.

In addition, the Target Chip Ganassi Racing Team donates $5,000 for each race the teams win as well as $1,000 per pole position and $25 for every lap led during the season. These contributions have amounted to as much as $75,000 in a single racing season.

Target House is publicized on in-store displays and other promotional materials, brochures, and pharmacy prescription bags, and has been featured in at least two of the company's national television commercials in an effort to raise awareness of the facility's existence and to invite public support. It is the retailer's ongoing effort to help sustain the program and do good in a way that will be remembered kindly by its customers.

Target still hopes to differentiate its pharmacies from those of its competitors. Creating a national branded program that its customers and employees can associate with the company, become involved with, and support through their purchases and contributions is one part of that effort.

St. Jude Children's Research Hospital's goal is to secure the needed funding for its operating and research costs and provide free housing to its patients and their families in a positive setting during periods of extended outpatient treatment. At the same time, it is trying to open new potential areas of funding by communicating the success of Target House.

As a cause marketing partnership, Target Stores and St. Jude Hospital hope to advance the cause of better children's health through biomedical research and continue to create free housing for St. Jude patients undergoing long-term treatment as well as for their families. Target House at St. Jude Hospital is a tangible reflection of some $12 million in funds raised or donated by Target. In return, Target has received favorable national media attention that has enhanced its corporate reputation, increased employee morale, and resulted in higher employee retention rates. The facility has helped the company achieve a greater level of awareness as a committed member of the community; and the company has also reported successful returns on its in-store pharmacy concept. In this case, a well-considered partnership achieved the goals each side had hoped for.

WHEN CORPORATE CULTURES FORM
THE RIGHT MARKETING MIX

Cause marketing should be about making a difference. As a rule, nonprofit corporations are created to help people and do good works, so the companies that sustain and enable these good works deserve to be rewarded in some way. The reward may be an increase in business or a jump in the company's stock price because its reputation is on the upswing. But ultimately, on a personal and corporate level, the real prize is when everybody wins—when everyone associated with the effort can say they feel better and are better for having been a part of it.

Timberland Company

The cause marketing partnership of Timberland Company and City Year is such an experience. Timberland is an international brand best known for its footwear, apparel, and accessories; City Year is a national youth service organization. The two began their relationship in 1989 and have since been described as demonstrating a "new paradigm" for corporate and nonprofit partnerships that extends beyond cause-related marketing to an entity fully integrated into the cultures of both organizations. Timberland has gone as far as opening a City Year office inside its own global headquarters in New Hampshire.

Founded in 1988, City Year brings together diverse young adults for a challenging year of full-time community service, leadership development, and civic engagement in 13 sites across the United States. The experience is designed to promote citizenship and social cohesion and at the same time to address local community needs. The founders of City Year, after witnessing several pieces of proposed national service legislation defeated in the 1980s, sought to secure private funding for a program that would make a meaningful difference in the lives of young people. They believed that the program could be developed with greater freedom using private funds and thus be free of government regulation.

The chief executive officer of Timberland recognized that City Year's mission paralleled his own personal commitment to community service and embodied his company's values—humanity, integrity, humility, and excellence. He also believed that Timberland's heritage of community investment, work-life balance, and a strong set of values would support the success of a partnership.

In the beginning, City Year approached Timberland about supplying the organization with products to outfit its members. The company agreed to do so and donated 70 pairs of Timberland work boots the first year and 100 pairs a year later. These were acts of generosity—corporate contributions that were not yet a cause marketing program but nonetheless a start on modestly helping the organization meet its needs.

After the second donation, one of City Year's founders visited Timberland's headquarters to make a presentation to the company's

CEO and other members of management. In outlining the organization's mission, goals, and fundraising philosophy at the time, he was asking companies to sponsor individual City Year service teams, which would use the sponsoring company's name. He also invited Timberland employees to participate in City Year community service activities.

The presentation proved to be the pivotal point in the development of the partnership, solidifying the company's desire to contribute to—and be affiliated with—the organization. Timberland agreed to sponsor a team and, over several years that followed, expanded the arrangement to include other activities. In 1995 the company became the founding national sponsor of City Year.

Timberland's social enterprises department manages the cause marketing partnership under a formal agreement that outlines the company's financial and product commitments. Staff from its social enterprises, marketing, communications, and product development departments—along with City Year brands and corporate managers, marketing and communications directors, and staff from the national affairs and development departments—attend most partnership meetings. Grants made by Timberland to City Year come from the company's Social Enterprise budget, which also pays administrative and staff costs for the program.

Under the company's volunteerism program, Path of Service, each Timberland employee receives 40 hours of annual paid leave to participate in service work or 3-month service sabbaticals to offer pro bono professional consultation to nonprofit organizations. Employees also participate in a number of service events organized for the company by City Year, such as the annual Serve-a-thon day of service, or employees can choose to volunteer elsewhere. The company provides consulting expertise, office space, uniforms, and other clothing to City Year corps members, in addition to leasing furnishings, supplies, and office space to the organization in at least two cities.

In 1995 Timberland began selling City Year Gear in its retail outlets. In 1999 the company began testing cobranded products and
merchandise, including a Timberland work boot in red, City Year's
signature color. In 2000 the red boot was successfully expanded to
seven markets, generating about $224,000 and enhancing the com-
pany's image as a result of greater awareness.

Timberland uses extensive in-store signage to promote the program, as well as to promote the red boot and other products in publicity campaigns that include print and radio ads in the markets
where the boots are sold. Timberland also includes information on
the cause marketing program in collateral materials, including the
annual *Corporate Social Responsibility Report* and *The Work,* a quar-
terly newsletter that highlights employee volunteerism and civic
leadership.

Timberland's goals are to become the reference brand for so-
ciably responsible campaigns; make community service a central
feature of the company's brand identity; provide value to the company's constituent groups through a corporate commitment to service; strengthen the communication, team building, and leadership
skills within the company; develop innovative business models that
create community wealth and sustainable change; and operate in a
manner consistent with the company's mission and values.

City Year hopes to expand its program across the United States,
increase the social impact of its service activities, build and enhance
its brand, and increase its visibility as well as the effectiveness and
efficiency of its business model through the expertise of, and mentoring by, Timberland employees.

Together, the partners in the cause marketing effort look to increase social justice, have an impact on community needs, and unify
diverse communities by expanding both the ethics and the services
they represent across the United States and around the world.

City Year has provided access to new markets for the company,
particularly in urban areas where the organization has both connections and credibility. Timberland was included on *Fortune* maga-

zine's list of the "100 Best Companies to Work For" (1997 to 2000) and received the 1998 Points of Light Foundation's Excellence in Corporate Community Service Award for its partnership with City Year and its involvement in service. The partnership helped City Year expand from 1 to 13 cities across America and from 50 to more than 1,000 corps members. Former U.S. President Bill Clinton said the organization was the model for the 1993 act that established AmeriCorps.

The cause marketing partnership of Timberland and City Year did what it was created to do—it advanced the profiles of the organizations behind it and focused on helping people and on leaving the world a little better for its having been there.

MARKETING FOR EDUCATION

Once upon a time kids were taught to eat a healthy breakfast before heading off to school. The advice remains the same today, only the kids are also told to remember to bring along the box tops from their breakfast cereal or their biscuit or pancake mix. The box tops aren't being saved for secret decoder rings or a similar extension of childhood fantasy. Now they are saved for cash. This change is not a modern-day story of the triumph of commerce over childhood; it is an example of powerfully effective cause marketing.

General Mills

General Mills is one of a number of the largest companies in the United States that recognize the value of cause marketing and are continually exploring ways of putting something back into the communities in which they do business and building good will with their customers. The company's chairman and CEO stated in the colorful, glossy 32-page *General Mills 2001 Corporate Citizenship Report:* "Caring about each other is an integral part of our company's culture, and partnering with our neighbors not only enriches lives but helps us understand and identify what we need to tackle next."

He might also add that what goes around comes around—that caring about each other keeps customers coming back and is very good for business.

What General Mills has tackled since at least 1995 is education— finding ways to help local schools on a continuing basis. Because funding for education is rarely able to keep pace with inflation (indeed, most schools are asked each year to do more with less), every school district or region has its own shortages, from paper to chalk or soccer balls to computers. There seldom seems enough in the budget for teachers or principals to do what they would like to do. In addition, every school or district has its priorities, and the debate over money for academics, art, sports, or the school playground seems never ending.

Under the General Mills Box Tops for Education program, how the company's help is provided is left up to the school. Box tops from any (or all) of more than 330 different General Mills products found in an average grocery store are worth money to the school in a plan as easy to understand as 1-2-3:

1. Clip the box tops from General Mills products.

2. Send the box tops to participating school.

3. Watch the school mailbox for a check from the company.

More than 65,000 schools, grades K through 8, enrolled in the program save box tops from products such as Cheerios, Chex, Trix, Go-Gurt, Hamburger Helper, Bisquick, Yoplait Yogurt, any Betty Crocker brand product, and hundreds of others. The school then collects the box tops and sends them to General Mills, which redeems them for 10¢ each, up to $10,000 per school year. With 65,000 participating schools, each one eligible to receive up to $10,000, the program's value to recipients is estimated up to $650 million per year.

The concept is simple: kids bring box tops from General Mills products to school and the schools redeem the box tops for cash—up to $30,000 per year per school. It's a textbook example of a company putting money back into local communities that help the company prosper by buying its products. (Photo by Karin Gottschalk Marconi)

The company believes the program has been so successful for these reasons:

- Participating is simple.

- It offers a "bilingual tool kit" to help schools create their own fundraising campaign.

- It delivers cash that the schools may then apply to their own unique needs.

- It provides opportunities to local schools in an uncomplicated way.

- It promotes team building among students, parents, educators, and the community.

Following its initial success, the program was expanded to include an Online Box Tops for Education Marketplace to capitalize on the growing use of computers by students, families, schools, and businesses. In the original program, schools received 10¢ for each box top redeemed. In the online extension, shoppers register at <boxtops4education.com> and each time a purchase is made online at <amazon.com>, <officemax.com>, <proflowers.com>, <eddie bauer.com>, or more than 100 other online sites, up to 10 percent of each qualifying purchase from an affiliated store is donated to the shopper's designated school up to $10,000 per school year.

An additional adaptation is using a General Mills Box Top for Education Visa Card, which allows 1 percent of every purchase amount to be sent to the cardholder's designated school up to $10,000 per school year. In this way, General Mills is helping schools raise money as people shop for everything from gas to major appliances (which are not General Mills products) at some 20 million locations where Visa cards are accepted.

Schools that encourage the use of all three ways to access the program could collect up to a total of $30,000 per school year. As this report is being compiled, more than 60 percent of U.S. schools are enrolled in the Box Tops for Education program, and more than half of America's households with children collect the box tops. In its first five years, more than $50 million had been distributed to schools through the program; in fact, the box tops sent to General Mills during March 2001 alone filled 11 tractor trailers.

In this instance, General Mills, a company that can well afford to do things its own way—it does not need a partner to help underwrite costs or provide issue management expertise—has set up and managed its own program through its marketing and public relations departments. Its cause is one that inarguably has a link to its products, its customers, and every community in which it does business. By including Visa and more than 100 online merchants in the program's expansion, it has broadened its reach, its visibility, and its benefits and yet has kept the costs of expansion to a minimum for the company and its new partners.

Not every company can undertake a cause marketing effort on such a scale, but as the expression goes, "Everything is relative." General Mills has provided a model for a local business to adapt to its own profile: define a local cause and create a "box top." The company's approach is efficient, simple. and smart.

UPS

The familiar brown trucks, brown uniforms, and shield logo on any given day are as close as the nearest office building lobby or traffic light. UPS (which is rarely called United Parcel Service, its original name) seems to be everywhere. The company built an excellent reputation as a package delivery and messenger service, based on efficient service, competitive pricing, and creating long-term relationships with its accounts. More perhaps than many other businesses, the package delivery service does not make money on one-time users. It logically follows then that the company has a unique understanding of the importance of building ties to the communi-

This ad promotes the "10th Annual National Association of Letter Carriers' Food Drive," which is sponsored by the letter carriers' employer, the U.S. Postal Service, and one of the oldest and most familiar labels in American kitchens, Campbell's Soup. It's a curious example of cause marketing, because while the event is clearly intended to focus attention on the issue of hunger, one day a year designated to "Stamp Out Hunger" seems odd. One might think local post offices could serve as drop-off points all year long and a giant food company would be a more active facilitator. If that is the case, it's not reflected in this ad, which underscores the need for effectively communicating the strongest message to benefit the cause marketing partners. (Photo by Karin Gottschalk Marconi)

ties it serves and identifying itself with constituents to whom brand loyalty means something.

In 1951 the UPS Foundation was created to, according to its mission statement, "act as a catalyst that promotes volunteer opportunities and provides support for education and urgent human needs through focused, funded initiatives."

The foundation's Community Investment Grants program "works on the principle that the more you invest, the greater the rewards." The foundation offers additional grants to causes in which UPS people have already volunteered more than 120 hours. This is a recognition that commitment of service should be supported where possible with funding, and committed funds should be supported by service in the form of volunteerism.

An example of UPS's cause marketing in an area of higher education is in its UNCF/UPS Corporate Scholars Program. The clumsy acronym in its name might be a minor disservice to its innovative approach. UPS entered into a partnership with the United Negro College Fund to provide unique opportunities to college students. The UNCF/UPS Corporate Scholars Program gives students a double opportunity: scholarships that provide essential financial support for college plus internships that offer real-world work experience. The program takes the position that by combining the two approaches to learning—the classroom and the corporate environment—the Corporate Scholars program provides each participating student a foundation for a successful career. A simple, yet imaginative, approach—school, a job, tuition plus expenses—is a real-life program that combines education and experience people can relate to on all levels.

UPS, however, understands that community service and community interests do not begin at college age. Grants to local elementary schools, supplemented by employees volunteering their time to read and act as mentors to school children, establishes a bond with a company and a respect from the community that promotes brand loyalty.

Hope Forberg, principal of Field Park Elementary School in Western Springs, Illinois, said a UPS grant makes a big difference in allocating already tight school budgets. But the participation is also important because such partnerships offer students increased educational resources by providing additional volunteers to read with students on a one-to-one basis or to teach them about the importance of saving money. The funding helps a lot, but the onsite personal commitment gets noticed in particular.

UPS has recognized that cause marketing makes sense. By going where people live and work to help and participate in the activities that are part of their life is good for business.

LIFE IN THE FAST LANE

For at least two generations, it has been said that Americans are having a love affair with their cars. Some people would argue that such romantic inclinations went beyond U.S. borders and were more a reflection of affluence and ego, but that is a debate for another time. This case summary is of an American car company's desire to show it cared about people as well as selling cars. It is also an illustration of a large international corporation building its "reservoir of goodwill" with a public that in recent times often regarded such corporations with suspicion and distrust.

Ford Motor Company

A theory holds that the larger and more successful a company, the more the public has a right to expect from it. That applies to a sense of social responsibility as well as quality, service, and value in what a company has to offer. This example shows a company with the resources to do something important for society coming forward and doing just that.

Apart from ongoing philanthropy through sponsorships, donations, and such entities as the Ford Foundation conferring grants over several decades to a wide variety of causes, the Ford Motor Company became involved in a cause marketing effort focused on a major, high-profile health issue. The issue was breast cancer, which because of the high percentage of women who fall victim to it was a highly visible health concern.

Ford is one of the oldest and most successful companies in the automobile industry. Known for producing a line of low-cost and mid-range family cars and trucks, Ford has had its share of rough rides over the years. For several years, the company ran an ad campaign with the theme "Ford has a better idea." When Ford began a successful cause marketing relationship aimed at responding to breast cancer, millions of people regarded it as one of the company's "better ideas" indeed.

While Ford's business was manufacturing stylish, road-safe vehicles the public would want to buy, this very significant commitment to breast cancer reflected a social conscience and a large-scale effort aimed at reaching out and saving lives in ways seat belts and air bags could not. In years to come, support and participation in such efforts helped to sustain Ford's reputation as a good corporate citizen and to exploit the goodwill it had built up with the public, its employees, and dealer network when questions about the company's commitment to public safety was questioned.

Traditionally, the purchase of an automobile has been a task performed by male family members. Even in female households, the opinion of fathers or brothers was sought regarding such purchases. With rare exceptions, the feeling was "cars are a guy thing." Additionally, Ford wanted to address what it believed was the commonly held misconception that it was a male brand.

To build credibility with women car buyers, the company believed it needed to change the way it communicated with women and to "fold women into its brand promise." To accomplish this ob-

jective, the company aligned itself with a cause that clearly demon-
strated its connection with—and commitment to—women.

For many women, breast cancer is a lifelong fear. A growing percentage of Ford's customers are women. That the company should
focus some of its attention on the issue made sense. In 1995, the
Ford Motor Company's Ford Division and the Susan G. Komen
Breast Cancer Foundation became partners in an effort to raise
awareness and resources to eradicate breast cancer.

The Komen Foundation is widely recognized as a leading organization supporting breast cancer research, education, screening,
and treatment. In addition, the Komen Foundation's Race for the
Cure events had local implications that would enable Ford dealer
groups, as well as individual dealers, to become actively involved at
the ground level. Ford and the Komen Foundation created a test of
the program's potential in Philadelphia in 1995. It has since been
expanded nationwide. From these beginnings, Ford's relationship
with the Komen Foundation has grown to become an integral part
of the company's belief system.

Over a six-year period, Ford donated $48 million to the founda-
tion in sponsorship fees, media support, and in-kind gifts. In addition, the number of Ford dealers participating in Komen Race for
the Cure events soared from 54 in 1995 to more than 3,000 in 2001.
The creation of the Ford Force served to leverage a united group of
Ford dealers, employees, and members of the general public in the
fight against breast cancer. As members of Ford Force, more than
12,000 Ford employees have participated in Komen Foundation
races across the United States.

Ford has a two-year agreement with the Komen Foundation un-
der which the auto company is a National Race Series sponsor.
Ford's marketing communications department manages the rela-
tionship with support from the J. Walter Thompson National Event
Team. J. Walter Thompson, a unit of the London-based WPP
Group, is the brand communications company that supports Ford's

communications program. Ford and Komen representatives have a monthly conference call and meet formally twice a year.

Much of the focus of efforts to combat breast cancer center on education and creating public awareness. Putting a personal face on the subject, in 1997 Ford underwrote an episode of the long-running and highly rated network television series *Murphy Brown*, a program with a large female audience and a history of addressing social concerns. In the series, the main character was dealing with breast cancer. As the sole advertiser of the episode, Ford donated three minutes of advertising time to Breast Cancer Public Service Announcements. At the conclusion of the television program, the Komen toll-free number (800-IMAWARE) and Web site (www .breastcancerinfo.com) reported dramatic increases in contacts from women with serious health questions.

Additionally, Ford developed several print media inserts with singer-actress Olivia Newton-John documenting her own battle with breast cancer and her association with the Komen Detroit Race for the Cure.

Research indicated that after reading the media inserts, some 19 percent of the readers (an estimated 37 million people) took action and scheduled a personal health examination. Readers also reported feeling better about Ford.

Ford also sponsored a special report on breast cancer in *People* magazine, in which 11 celebrities who were survivors of breast cancer shared their personal stories. They included Ms. Newton-John, former First Lady Betty Ford, Julia Child, Shirley Temple, and skating star Peggy Fleming. The report also included inspirational stories of women who were *not* celebrities. This edition of *People* reached more than 34 million people, an estimated 22 million of whom were women.

Understanding the importance of reaching a younger female audience, Ford featured the cast of the hit television series *The Practice* in a similar print insert, in which the show's stars shared their stories and fears about breast cancer. This insert included postcards that readers could mail to family and friends, encouraging them to get a mammogram or to attend a Komen Race for the Cure event.

In 2000, Ford also partnered with television's Lifetime Cable Network—a network whose trademarked ad slogan is "Television for Women"—in support of Breast Cancer Awareness Month in October. The auto company sponsored a public awareness campaign with a tag line that directed the audience to a Ford Force Web site for a sweepstakes entry. Between September 4 and November 15, the Web site recorded more than 122,000 visitors.

In 2001, Ford involved the fashion community in its awareness campaign, enlisting a rising fashion designer to create a new bandanna aimed at showing solidarity in the fight against breast cancer. The designer bandannas were given to everyone participating in Ford-sponsored events and widely distributed through a retail partnership with Macy's East and Macy's West department stores.

The Ford name was visible on tents, banners, and bandannas at all Komen Race for the Cure events. In 12 races, the company featured a "Capture the Passion" digital photo opportunity for participants who could then access their photos on a Ford company Web site.

As the Internet became a frequently accessed source for information, Ford helped fund an award-winning Web site—www.fordvehi cles.com/fordcares/fordforce—that offered information on breast cancer and local Komen Race for the Cure events.

Ford dealers and dealer groups contributed more than $5 million in 2000, providing cash sponsorships, advertising, in-kind materials, and services in support of some 100 local Komen Race for the Cure events. Commercials for local events are financed through local Ford dealers' advertising budgets. One dealer, in order to bring the event to his community, formed his own 501(c)(3) Race for the Cure affiliate organization. Dealer support for the program soared from an initial 54 participating dealers in 1995 to more than 3,000 in

2001. More than 12,000 of the company's employees have participated by running or walking in the events across the United States.

The Ford Motor Company set goals of forming lasting, emotional connections between women and the Ford brand; becoming involved in something that matters to its customers; and demonstrating its commitment to social responsibility as a core corporate value. Its own analysis of its partnership with the Komen Foundation indicates the effort has had a positive impact on its image, as well as on consumer purchase decisions. A consumer survey in the year 2000 revealed that 75 percent of those surveyed felt better about Ford, and 29 percent were more likely to consider purchasing the company's product as a result of its involvement with the cause. In 2001, some 4,000 Ford employees participated in Detroit, and nationally more employees are involved than ever before.

The Komen Foundation's goals for the partnership were to eradicate breast cancer; leverage Ford's extensive distribution network to reach a broader and more varied target market; and achieve greater reach and visibility for both the foundation and the race series through Ford's powerful branding, advertising, and public relations activities. Komen credits its partnership with Ford for contributing to the steady, impressive growth of its Komen Race for the Cure events, making it the largest series of 5K runs in the world. It continues to grow by an estimated 39 percent each year. After several of Ford's public service announcements, the Komen Web site and toll-free number reported increased usage among women with serious health questions. Research indicated several of Ford's advertising inserts in women's magazines resulted in a more than 19 percent increase in readers scheduling breast examinations in 1998 and 2000.

Ford's partnership with the Komen Foundation took advantage of formula tactics that used print media, broadcast and cable television, Internet sites, event marketing, and celebrity participants, and the approach proved effective in creating awareness of its cause. The shared goal of the partners was to increase breast cancer awareness and early detection among women of all age groups. Through a strategic alignment stressing the importance of a strong connection between the brand and the cause; a topical message carefully targeted to specific demographic groups; cross-cultural communications that delivered the campaign's message to diverse audiences; and local community involvement, the effort proved to be highly effective.

Ford indicated it planned to continue its relationship with the Komen Foundation beyond sponsorship to an ongoing cause marketing partnership.

AND LEAVE THE WORLD A BETTER PLACE

Large, successful companies are encouraged to allocate some of their considerable resources for the greater public good, and many of them do as a matter of social responsibility or simply because it seems to make good business sense. But not every company is large, nor does it have deep pockets or available resources that can make a major difference on the larger public landscape. Yet, idealism— a social conscience and a desire to truly make the world a better place—is not a function of size. A concern for the environment and the future of the planet reflects an idealism that, despite an increase of public cynicism, is alive and well in the United States and around the world. Smaller companies, guided by idealistic, committed individuals, are making a difference, often one small step at a time.

Grabber Performance Group

To many people, Grabber Performance Group is not only *not* a household name among American companies, it also is not especially known at all outside of its industry. However, it is a company with a mission, and if its mission is successful, everybody wins.

Grabber, a division of John Wagner Associates, Inc., is the largest distributor of hand, pocket, and toe warmers in North America. Although considered a small or midsized company by business standards, the contributions Grabber has made have been significant. Its primary product—an odorless, nontoxic, biodegradable warming sachet—is used mostly in gloves, pockets, and shoes.

Noting that warmth can be generated in two forms—one through science, the other through the compassion of the human heart—the company's founders created the Share the Warmth partnership program as a way to unite the two forms. Through Share the Warmth, Grabber has had an impact on a variety of environmental and humanitarian causes, including Habitat for Humanity, AmeriCares, and various community and individual programs and organizations.

The primary environmental component of Share the Warmth is Grabber's ten-year involvement with the Conservation Alliance, an effort it was instrumental in both creating and sustaining. Grabber's involvement with the Conservation Alliance allows it to protect, preserve, and restore the very thing that is central to its business—the outdoors. Other efforts that are part of Share the Warmth promote humanitarian causes.

The program grew out of a 1989 meeting held at an outdoor industry trade show. The former CEOs of REI Co-op and The North Face felt that companies in the outdoor industry were not doing enough to promote environmental awareness. With the help of the owners of other environmentally conscious companies—namely Patagonia and Kelty—a meeting was convened with leaders from the companies attending the conference to discuss mutual environmental interests and concerns. With nearly 200 people in attendance, the CEO of the REI Co-op proposed that the leaders form a coalition to protect the environment and that each member contribute $10,000. This coalition evolved into what is now the Conservation Alliance. Ron Nadeau, founder and co-owner of Grabber Performance Group, was first to pledge support for the Conservation Alliance and has been an active member ever since.

As it evolved, the Conservation Alliance has revised its membership fee structure so that companies of any size can now become a part of the effort. The Alliance grew to 70 members, who each year contributed $1,000 per $1 million of revenue, with a suggested cap of $10,000. In addition, member companies staff the Alliance, enabling 100 percent of donated funds to be given to charitable causes. The Conservation Alliance awards approximately ten grants of $25,000 to $35,000 annually to small grassroots environmental groups.

Grabber's cause marketing effort is managed by its marketing department with participation from the company's operations and sales staffs. For many years, Ron Nadeau publicly downplayed Grabber Performance Group's giving practices out of concern that they might be perceived as having a "give-to-get" agenda. Now that Grabber has an established history of supporting charitable causes, its executives feel more comfortable with their social message being told.

The Conservation Alliance logo appears in all of Grabber's advertising and on all the company's products and literature. Reps, distributors, and both wholesale and retail customers of the company know that a percentage of sales are allocated to the Alliance and other nonprofit organizations through the Share the Warmth program. Grabber brings its environmental message to the consumer as well. All products include the message "Be Responsible" under an image of the planet earth. Using the Conservation Alliance in the United States as the model, similar alliances have been established in Australia and Japan.

Another component of Grabber's Share the Wealth program involves the company forming partnerships with some of its retail customers to support local Habitat for Humanity programs. The partnership involves a percentage of sales or matching funds. Donations are made by Grabber on behalf of the retailer. Grabber also is known for giving away tree saplings at trade shows to advertise its support of the Conservation Alliance. Nadeau believes that by giving away a live tree, which recipients must then plant and care for, Grabber is promoting a more lasting message of environmental responsibility. In support of Share the Warmth programs, Grabber Performance Group has donated hand warmers to Kosovo and Mongolian relief efforts. The approximate value of the donation is $145,000.

The head of Grabber Performance Group also encourages the development of partnership alliances and educational programs for consumers, both inside Grabber and at other organizations. Support of the Conservation Alliance and other social causes is communicated through industry events, press releases, magazine articles, and interviews. The effort is the subject of a book, *The Conservation Alliance: Making a Difference,* by Amy Irvine, a noted rock climber, ski guide, wilderness advocate, and freelance writer. She documented the good works in support of the Conservation Alliance and other social causes that are normally communicated through industry events, press releases, magazine articles, and interviews. Information about the Conservation Alliance and Grabber's philanthropic initiatives are highlighted on both organizations' Web sites.

Grabber's goals for its program initially were to invest in mutually beneficial and enduring relationships with its employees, customers, vendors, and the communities in which the Company does business. It also hoped to make the Grabber brand name synonymous with Share the Warmth, while increasing profits by fulfilling customers' needs. Grabber further wanted to grow its business in order to deepen its philanthropic efforts. It also hoped to be regarded as a company with a product that reminded people of giving from the heart—inspiring others to be kinder, more compassionate, and generous. The company continues to develop environmentally sustainable products and solutions through research, innovation, and new technologies.

Many cause marketing partnerships involve a company and a nonprofit organization coming together out of mutual need for mutual benefit. Grabber is a company whose leaders were guided by a social conscience that envisioned and created a program and an alliance to do good. The results of the effort were that Grabber's Share the Warmth program has helped to build a core ideology and a greater sense of purpose for the company. In addition, company representatives believe Grabber's social programs have contributed to increased employee loyalty and stronger relationships with retailers and customers.

The Conservation Alliance has been able to preserve, protect, and restore thousands of acres of free-flowing waterways and trails, several million acres of wild lands, and numerous species of flora and fauna. Grants from the Alliance—some $3.2 million between 1990 and 2000—have been used to support congressional lobbying efforts to curb logging practices and gain permanent protection for the California Headwaters Forest, as well as to help the Inter-Tribal Sinkyone lands in California and establish the nation's first intertribal wilderness park there. Together, the partners hoped to also preserve, protect, and restore the outdoors and raise awareness of the need for businesses to be socially responsible.

Grabber faced a major challenge in that differences existed in corporate parent management priorities. The views of John Wagner Associates differed from those of Grabber, its subsidiary. A further challenge was that Grabber's advertising and promotions budget was limited.

Grabber intends to continue its relationship with the Conservation Alliance indefinitely. The Company contributes approximately $5,000 to $12,000 per year to the Conservation Alliance, not including in-kind gifts and other expenses. Grabber's founder, who was the initial driving force behind Share the Warmth, believes that the success of the program comes from the shared sense of values and commitment to change by others in the company.

The philosophy holds that the creation of alliances and relation-ships can produce powerful sources of energy and ideas for change, and an idea founded on a "higher" cause or goal, followed by two or more people joining to take action, can lead to social transfor-mation or impact a cause.

Grabber Performance Group plans to expand its social message to consumers and all levels of distribution, sales, and marketing with the goal of increasing brand recognition. The company's man-agement hopes to inspire its product users to Share the Warmth with others for the benefit of environmental and humanitarian causes. A small company with a big plan has ambitions to do well by doing good.

OFFLINE, HELP OF ANOTHER KIND

Being a good corporate citizen should be an ongoing, everyday activity. Yet, in times of tragedy, local businesses are tested. A trag-edy of the magnitude of September 11, 2001, when terrorists tar-geted U.S. cities and the media provided minute-by-minute accounts of the rescue and relief efforts, is not an everyday occurrence. How-ever, communities are struck by tragedy when the world is *not* watch-ing and the media pays little more than casual notice—despite the fact that lives are lost, buildings destroyed, and businesses and the jobs and stability they represent are obliterated. Terrorist attacks shock and outrage. Fires, floods, hurricanes, and tornadoes that leave communities devastated are accepted as a fact of life. To the companies committed to the communities in which they operate, these devastating events are larger than life.

Compaq

Compaq Computer Corporation is a Fortune Global 100 com-pany and a leading international provider of technology solutions. The company designs, develops, manufactures, and markets hardware, software, solutions, and services, including a line of products sold in more than 200 countries. In 2002, Compaq was at the center of a boardroom storm, as opposing factions of Hewlett-Packard (HP) shareholders raged at each other over whether or not management's announced plan to purchase Compaq was a good thing or a bad thing for HP.

A year earlier, Compaq had been in the path of another storm, but there was not much debate about that one. It was called tropical storm Allison and its effects proved devastating to Houston, Texas, and the greater Houston area. Houston is the worldwide headquarters of Compaq Computer.

In June of 2001, Allison dumped up to 36 inches of rain on the Houston area during one five-day siege that ended June 9. Final reports said thousands were left homeless. An estimated 2,744 homes and nearly 700 mobile homes were destroyed. In all, more than 43,000 county residents experienced some damage. Approximately 400 employees of Compaq felt the storm's impact personally.

In the midst of this upheaval, Compaq had a business to run. Around the world, customers expected orders to be filled and products to be delivered. The company had obligations. Yet, despite its position as a major global company, Compaq also was part of a community made up of people whose lives were being changed, in some cases, washed away. And management believed the company also had an obligation to its Houston friends and family.

Compaq's response to the disaster came in many forms, including cash, technology, in-kind contributions, and volunteers, as well as employee cash loan programs and community equipment purchase programs. Internal organizations that took part in the effort included Employee Communications, Corporate Community Relations, Real Estate and Operating Services, Investment Recovery, North America Government Education Markets, Human Resource Benefits, Human Resources IM, the Compaq Factory Outlet, Remarketing Group, and DemoPaq. Some 900 local Compaq employees volunteered and employees of the company from sites around the United States collected clothing and dry goods that were sent to Houston.

The company wanted to help its own people but offered help to the larger community as well—a $50,000 cash contribution for disaster relief to the Red Cross' Houston Area Chapter; $40,000 in equipment to the Federal Emergency Management Agency (FEMA); $10,000 in cash to Northwest Assistance Ministries' disaster relief; $10,000 in equipment to Reach Out America for disaster relief efforts; and donations of $17,500 and $10,000 in equipment, respectively, to the Alley Theatre and the Society for the Performing Arts to replace equipment that had been damaged or destroyed by the storm.

Compaq announced that it would replace flood-damaged computers at any school, college, and state or local agency in Houston at no profit to the company. The offer applied not only to Compaq computers that were damaged as a result of the flood but also to any manufacturer's equipment. The company also encouraged its employees to donate blood and initiated a dollar-for-dollar match program in which employees were told that Compaq would match donations of $50 or more made by U.S.-based employees through the Compaq Matching Gift program to the Red Cross Greater Houston Chapter for Flood Relief. Compaq's public statement read in part: "The Houston Flood was another example of employee generosity to help others less fortunate."

Employees did rise to the occasion, but the company as an organization looked very good as well. To provide immediate aid to people most in need, on top of its $50,000 to the local Red Cross chapter, Compaq delivered three generators to a local hospital to keep it up and running and set up a flood relief command center on its corporate campus to serve as a supply drop-off and distribution location. The company also provided a facility to serve as a Salvation Army Distribution Center. Special programs were set up to provide financial assistance, food, furniture, clothing, and other items to help Compaq's own employees whose homes were hit by the disaster. It was noted that the company regularly engaged in various team-building activities, and its people proved in this situation how well they had been paying attention.

Certainly other businesses and corporations in the area contributed money and equipment, volunteered, and assisted in relief efforts—and some did not. This case is noteworthy for three reasons:

1. Compaq is a major international technology company.

2. People in the technology industry, from senior management to junior programmers, are often represented as arrogant and detached from matters of social concern.

3. The tropical storm and flood it left behind occurred at a time when the computer industry was being hit hard economically by job cuts and closings that were creating their own brand of financial wreckage for thousands of industry people who were already experiencing their own kinds of personal disasters.

Compaq Computer's response to the situation in Houston suggests the company's management did not have to vote on what its priorities would be. It understood that the concept of good corporate citizenship meant more than its ongoing relationship with United Way and contributions to some local charities. Corporate social responsibility involves being a company the community can count on when times are hard.

WHEN OPPOSITES ATTRACT . . . FOR AWHILE

One of the basic points on the cause marketing partnership checklist is the importance of compatibility between the company and the nonprofit organization—a point that seems as if it should be fairly obvious. For unlikely partners to form a relationship can result in additional attention to the program. It is noteworthy because a surprise matchup is always newsworthy.

Another perspective on the issue falls under the heading of "marriage of convenience"—a partnership where each side has something the other side wants or needs and agrees to explore ways to work together without compromising commitments to each partner's separate position.

Mattel

In 1999, Mattel, arguably the largest toy company in the United States and maker of the hugely successful Barbie doll—began a cause marketing partnership with Girls Incorporated (formerly Girls Clubs of America), a national research, education, and advocacy organization. Many market observers thought the arrangement was an odd one in that the image of Barbie had been built around glamour, fashion, and luxury. Barbie's often frivolous, fun persona seemed at odds with an entity dedicated to empowering girls to become educated and involved in making the world a better place, regardless of curves and hairstyles. But the very goal of the partnership was to use the Barbie brand to provide girls with empowering messages, products, and educational materials that would inspire them to be strong, smart, and bold.

For its part, Mattel hoped to create an enhanced, more relevant Barbie brand through an association with a progressive, girl-focused organization. The company also wanted to reach a greater number of consumers by developing new Barbie concepts using research developed by Girls Inc. for a targeted demographic. Mattel, conscious of Barbie's image among more serious-minded individuals, wanted to help the Barbie brand gain acceptance and credibility among new constituencies and organizations.

Girls Inc. wanted to reach a million girls a year with its message of empowerment and advance its advocacy mission by partnering with a company that had established marketing capabilities and channels of distribution to the market it sought to reach. The organization also hoped to distribute its educational products and programs on a significantly larger scale, enhance its own brand identity, and gain visibility for its mission. It aimed to establish financial support to build organizational capacity and develop new products and dissemination mechanisms to advance its work. Additionally, Girls Inc. hoped that by sharing its research and expertise about the target market with Mattel, it might be able to influence the design and marketing of Barbie products, which had such a great influence on young girls.

So, the partnership was designed to enhance Mattel's Barbie brand image while spreading Girls Inc.'s message of empowerment to millions of girls around the world. Mattel distributes Girls Inc.'s educational materials with Barbie products and special events, and Girls Inc. provides Mattel with research and expertise about girls to help the company develop new product ideas.

In past years, Mattel organized charity programs associated with the introduction of each year's unique career-themed Barbie. However, the company did not believe these programs generated sufficient ongoing recognition for its philanthropic activities among Barbie customers. The decision to form a strategic, long-term partnership with a single organization and develop a program that would be highly visible and make a significant contribution to a cause was intended to change that. Mattel also saw value in a partnership with a girl-focused organization that would allow the company to support its primary constituency and provide access to new customers.

Girls Inc. was aware that it needed to seek nontraditional sources of funding to achieve its goal of broadening its audience and was considering developing a strategic marketing group. The director of the Mattel Foundation was familiar with Girls Inc. and recommended the organization as a potential partner. Mattel's head of public relations approached the organization in 1996. At the time, Girls Inc. did not have any corporate partnerships and recognized the fact that Mattel was not an obvious choice. It was well known that Barbie, while a hugely successful product for generations, had long been considered contrary to the Girls Inc. mission of empowering girls. But Barbie had such broad recognition and influence with girls that Girls Inc. recognized a partnership could increase its audience.

The nonprofit organization invited Mattel representatives to a Girls Inc. event to learn more about its goals, mission, and values. This experience solidified the toy company's desire to find a way to work with the organization. Nonetheless, like Girls Inc., Mattel had to overcome organizational resistance to forming a partnership with a feminist advocacy organization. The cautious and thoughtful relationship developed slowly. The internal consensus-building process took two years and included face-to-face meetings between Mattel's CEO and the national executive director of Girls Inc. Ultimately, the two organizations reached an agreement and formalized a three-year partnership pact in 1999.

That agreement outlined the "spirit" of the partnership and listed both parties' objectives, as well as specific guidelines related to such issues as the term of the partnership, financial commitment, intellectual property rights, use of the company's and the nonprofit organization's names and logos, and the decision-making process.

At Mattel, the company's director of public relations was designated to serve as the primary liaison to Girls Inc., with responsibility for managing the relationship. Members of the marketing, research, and promotions departments, as well as product managers for specific dolls tied to the program, were to be involved as needed. Mattel senior management, including the company's CEO, would participate in special events and promotions. A donation to Girls Inc. would come from the Barbie brand's corporate giving budget, while additional funds for marketing, special events, and product-related promotions would come from the associated department budgets.

At Girls Inc., the organization's director of development was to
have ultimate responsibility for the partnership and be Mattel's primary contact. An account manager would have day-to-day responsibility for coordinating the relationship. Meetings of the two staffs
took place about once each month, more frequently when special
events or product launches were underway.

The components of the cause marketing plan developed for
Mattel and Girls Inc. included product promotions, information
sharing, corporate philanthropy, special events, and a variety of
communication mechanisms, such as promoting the effort on the
packaging of specially created Barbie/Girls Inc. products. These
products sought to take maximum advantage of the power of the
Barbie franchise—a vast constituency of girls drawn to anything
bearing the Barbie name—while being true to the nonprofit organization's mission to empower girls.

The first promotion under the arrangement included a "Working Woman" career Barbie doll that came with information about
Girls Inc. on its highly identifiable packaging and in product ads,
as well as on the CD-ROM that was part of the package. The staff
of Girls Inc. shared its research findings and expertise with Mattel
and led training programs and workshops with Barbie product
designers, educating them in such matters as attitudes and preferences of girls today.

Girls Inc. reported—even in the early stages of the program—that
the partnership with Mattel had increased the visibility of the organization and had resulted in positive feedback about the partnership from other donors. This was viewed as helping to strengthen
the organization's fundraising base.

Mattel noted that the most tangible results had been what it regarded as favorable coverage of the partnership in the media. The
company believed its association with Girls Inc. would foster goodwill among consumers by publicizing the company's contributions
to an organization that helps girls.

Was the motivation of Mattel and Girls Inc. for participating in a cause marketing effort self-serving? Sure. This particular example does not aim to eradicate world hunger or solve the problems of the homeless or people who are terminally ill or provide relief to families whose homes were destroyed. However, it does partner a giant toy company that wanted to improve its product's brand image and market base with an organization that aimed to teach and motivate young girls to achieve their maximum potential. Barbie, it seems, had begun taking herself a bit more seriously and, as a marketing strategy, that was a good idea. Before the original three-year agreement ran its course, it was not extended. No matter how well intended, every cause marketing partnership is not necessarily forever.

WHEN THE CAUSE IS CHILDREN

Any company of any size in any industry can find some cause that will help it to define itself as a socially responsible good corporate citizen. Whether its aims are strictly business oriented, such as sponsoring a chair at a favored university's school of business, or more broadly directed, such as funding an environmental program from which everyone would benefit, society and the world have enough issues that anyone wishing to help can find a place.

Certainly, some causes involve what must be considered "hot button" issues—AIDS research, gun control, and family planning, for example—that stir the deepest passions and prejudices. Involvement in these types of issues and causes will surely register dramatically with split constituencies, winning deep loyalty and support from some, rejection and derision from others. Companies that take on controversial causes must understand the risk-reward ratios and choose accordingly, considering the impact their decisions will have on their investors, employees, and other stakeholders, as well as the business itself. A corporate social conscience is a brave, noble, moral, and potentially explosive quality.

The issue of better health care is an important and controversial matter in a large, diverse world community. Better health care for children—particularly very seriously ill children—seems to be a cause no one would find objectionable. It is also a cause in which a retail giant sought to make a meaningful difference, if only for a limited time.

Wal-Mart

In the year 2002, Wal-Mart was not only designated the leading retailer but also won the title of largest company in the world. That is not a title to which every business aspires and, of course, few are ever in contention. Nonetheless, it is worth noting where the world's largest company weighs in on cause marketing.

Wal-Mart founder Sam Walton's corporate philosophy was that companies have a responsibility to give back to the communities in which they do business. He certainly did not invent that phrase (or philosophy), but his company practiced it without qualification.

Wal-Mart's choice as a cause marketing partner was an entity that focused on two of life's major concerns—children and health care.

Children's Miracle Network (CMN) is an international not-for-profit organization dedicated to raising funds for and awareness of children's hospitals. Wal-Mart is CMN's largest corporate partner, having raised more than $160 million for the organization's network of 170 member hospitals since the partnership began in 1988. The Wal-Mart/CMN partnership model was designed so that fundraising programs are developed by and dedicated to local communities where both entities had a presence.

Since CMN was created in 1982, the organization has subscribed to the philosophy that nonprofits need to look beyond traditional sources of funding. In particular, CMN has sought to capitalize on the fundraising potential of corporate partnerships. In the early 1980s, the organization began developing partnerships with package goods manufacturers and major retailers, believing that such programs would provide greater visibility for the organization and open new avenues of funding.

CMN was aware of Sam Walton's philosophy, which made Wal-Mart a logical potential retail partner for CMN. In 1987, the co-founders of CMN met with Sam Walton to discuss a possible relationship. Such a prospect appealed to the retail giant because of the community-specific aspect of the hospital network. Supporting CMN would allow Wal-Mart to make a major difference in many of the communities where it operated. The company also saw the partnership as a good match with its commitment to children's health as a universal issue that appealed to all Wal-Mart customers and associates. Additionally, CMN's fundraising structure, in which 100 percent of funds raised by individual Wal-Mart stores would stay in those specific communities to support local hospitals, held strong appeal for the company. Wal-Mart agreed to develop a partnership and become a CMN corporate sponsor.

While the organization had contracts detailing specific funding commitments, program length, and a variety of other legal issues with other corporate sponsors, Wal-Mart and CMN have never had a formal agreement. The organization believed the corporate culture created by Sam Walton, which truly values community involvement, enabled the relationship between the two entities to develop differently than with other CMN sponsors. From the outset, CMN believed Wal-Mart was genuinely committed to the issue of children's health care and that a formal agreement might have limited or stifled the relationship.

While it was unusual for agreements of such magnitude to be unwritten, it was also a very basic premise of cause marketing that companies and organizations committed to such efforts be ethical and socially responsible. The Wal-Mart Foundation designated a community project manager and one other staff member to work on the CMN campaign and serve as the organization's key contacts. Other Wal-Mart departments were to be involved on an as-needed basis to support specific programs and promotions. The

Wal-Mart Foundation pays the administrative costs of the program. The company's marketing department funds advertising and Wal-Mart's senior vice chairman serves on CMN's board of governors.

The program operated regionally. Local stores worked with local hospitals, developing programs for their communities. Each Wal-Mart store had a community involvement leader, often a store employee who has volunteered to manage the store's community involvement program, though in some cases the community involvement leader was a paid staff person.

At CMN's national headquarters in Salt Lake City, one senior-level staff person was responsible for managing the partnership and involving other staff members as needed. Each CMN hospital in the national network employed a fundraising and marketing professional to manage the hospital's CMN relationships in the community. That person coordinated the program's activities directly with the hospital's local Wal-Mart stores.

When the relationship with Wal-Mart began, CMN was not well known nationally. Both Wal-Mart and CMN had to invest their time and resources to educate people about the organization. Because Wal-Mart was such a disproportionately large sponsor of CMN, providing some six times the funding of the organization as its next largest contributor, CMN continually explores new and creative ways to adequately recognize Wal-Mart's contribution without discouraging other corporate partners.

The Wal-Mart Foundation made an annual grant of $100,000 to the CMN national headquarters to cover the program's administration costs. Wal-Mart also named CMN as one of its official national corporate sponsorship programs. As such, the Wal-Mart Foundation agreed to match the first $1,000 that each store raised for CMN through local fundraising activities. The company did not commit to a minimum or maximum donation each year. In 1999, Wal-Mart raised and donated a total of $29 million to CMN.

Wal-Mart and CMN shared an objective: improving the quality of children's health care. Wal-Mart wanted to make a substantial contribution to the communities and at the same time develop a program that would allow its associates and customers to feel directly involved in making a contribution to a cause.

CMN's goal was to create corporate partnerships to support its hospitals in fulfilling their mission to help children, and ensure that these partnerships did not exploit children or promote products that had a negative effect on children. The organization also wanted to build awareness of the CMN hospital network in order to increase funding opportunities for its programs.

Wal-Mart raised and donated a total of $160 million for CMN. Both sides believed the partnership had a tremendous positive impact on children's health care. In many communities, local hospitals received $300,000 to $400,000 through the program each year, and some hospitals receive more than $500,000 annually. In many instances, local Wal-Mart stores' donations funded new equipment, health care programs, and services that might otherwise not have existed.

For several years, Wal-Mart believed its association with Children's Miracle Network improved the public's perception of the company in many of the communities in which it operates. Further, the company indicated the partnership had a positive impact on morale among associates in its organization. The 1999 Cone/Roper Cause Related Trends Report cited Wal-Mart as the company most frequently mentioned as a "good corporate citizen" by survey respondents.

The company's philosophy of giving something back to its communities was best illustrated in its commitment to children's health care in those communities.

But as BSR contacted Wal-Mart in 2001, the company reported that it had ended its partnership arrangement with Children's Miracle Network and, indeed, was no longer involved in company-initiated cause marketing efforts. Its four years of good work and what seemed to be goodwill were abruptly terminated. The company, it appeared, was rethinking its policies. Even the seemingly most successful programs are subject to change as corporate "winds" shift.

CAUSE MARKETING SNAPSHOTS

Various companies and organizations argue over who actually "invented" cause marketing and which entity has used it most effectively, but the fact remains that it is a concept that works on many levels for enterprises of virtually any size in almost any industry or category. Some may argue that a company giving its shareholders' money to charity is in conflict with the capitalistic system. That might be the subject for another book, but for this one the case is pretty clear. Companies that overtly help to support a worthwhile cause that benefits the community in which it does business wins the recognition, respect, loyalty, and support for itself from that community (and perhaps many other communities, both near and far). Such an effort is clearly good for business and, many would argue, good for society.

In some additional examples, briefly noted below, of other cause marketing efforts, both large and small, the results speak for themselves.

- The Walt Disney Company and the American Society for the Prevention of Cruelty to Animals (ASPCA) entered into more than 100 merchandising agreements that the ASPCA claims will be worth many millions of dollars to the organization over time. The organization is able to fund its animal protection and welfare efforts, while Disney lists its support for a cause that is largely admired by its family audience.

- MCI donates a percentage of its revenues from business customers to the Nature Conservancy or the Audubon Society in ongoing efforts to pacify nature lovers and dampen their adversarial feelings toward a technology company.

- Microsoft and AARP are partners in Lifetime Connection seminars, a program to educate older adults about personal computers. Research indicates that older people as a market segment are perhaps the group least excited about technology. Microsoft, which has several company-linked foundations, annually funds a wide variety of causes, such as providing libraries with equipment and expertise to bring more libraries online. AARP's membership is enormous, and Microsoft, often regarded as a very arrogant company, needs every friend it can get.

- Country singer Faith Hill established the Faith Hill Literacy Project, and fans attending her concerts are asked to donate a book to the project. So far, she has collected more than 1 million books plus cash and contributions from Southland Stores, owner of the 7-11 stores, to help promote the cause of literacy. The cause is worthy and Hill's reputation for caring about people who care about her is enhanced.

- Aetna Insurance and U.S. Healthcare designated $7 million to educate women about heart disease and stroke. Insurance companies are among the more disliked and distrusted businesses on most lists of consumer opinions. This type of effort helps neutralize the charge that insurance companies care about profits more than people.

- HBO featured naturalist Jane Goodall in commercials to attract new subscribers to its cable television network. Under normal circumstances, this would have simply been a case of an advertiser hiring a celebrity presenter. However, in this case the payment was made for her services to the Jane Goodall Institute and covered that organization's expenses for a year.

- The founder of Wendy's fast-food restaurants, the late Dave Thomas, established the Dave Thomas Foundation for Adoption. According to the *New York Times*, Wendy's "promoted the creation of innovative employment benefit programs for people who adopt, among other initiatives. Posters and tray liners in Wendy's restaurants each November promote the cause of adoption."

- American Express's activities in cause marketing are many and varied. As a sponsor of the San Francisco Arts Festival, the company gave 2¢ to the festival for every purchase charged on the American Express card. The experience proved successful, so the company expanded the concept to other markets; on a national level it promised to donate money to the Statue of Liberty/Ellis Island Foundation every time one of its cardholders used the card for a purchase. Even though American Express turned over $1.7 million to the foundation, it spent a reported $6 million publicizing its involvement. Its contribution was undoubtedly generous, but purists suggested it might have been better if the foundation had received the $6 million, and $1.7 million had been spent on American Express publicity. Despite the controversy, numerous worthy causes have benefited from the company's programs. The argument for true commitment to a cause as opposed to cause marketing for publicity purposes should top the agenda at a company's meeting to draft the plan.

- Tom's of Maine is known to its customers and employees as something more special than just another toothpaste company. The company gives 10 percent of its pretax profits to nonprofit organizations benefiting the environment, human need, arts, and education. Among the company's noteworthy grants is $500,000 to the Nature Conservancy toward the acquisition and preservation of 185,000 acres along the Upper St. John River, the longest free-flowing river east of the Mississippi. The company's mission, written collaboratively with its employees in 1989, attempts "to express in words what we feel in our own hearts should be (and are) the guiding principles of a company that seeks to promote the Common Good while pursuing a profit."

- The Body Shop "is a values-driven, high-quality skin and body care retailer operating in 50 countries with over 1,900 outlets." In 1999 it was voted the most trusted brand in the United Kingdom by the Consumers Association, and a 1998 survey of international chief executives, published in the *Financial Times* in 1998, ranked it the 27th most respected company in the world. The Body Shop Foundation's stated purpose "is to give financial support to pioneering front line organizations who have little hope of conventional funding" in efforts on behalf of human and civil rights and environmental and animal protection. Brash and controversial with no advertising, an in-your-face approach to public relations, and never reluctant to interrupt a sales pitch with a social commentary, The Body Shop has its critics, but the company also has its passionately loyal customers in every major country around the world.

- Ben & Jerry's makes and sells ice cream, but it was one of the earliest companies to gain national attention more for using its ice cream cartons to make a case for social and environmental causes. The company seemed to stop just short of claiming its premium-priced products were merely devices for presenting issues to a growing and curious following, for social issue fundraising, and for . . . cause marketing. The mission of Ben & Jerry's Foundation's is "to make the world a little better place by empowering Ben & Jerry's employees to use available resources to support and encourage organizations that are working toward eliminating the underlying causes of environmental and social problems."

The Body Shop built a worldwide business in personal care products, to a great degree through cause-related marketing. With virtually no ad budget and aiming its marketing effort toward a core constituency of people committed to a safe environment and opposed to using animals for product testing, the company has grown rapidly in terms of franchises sold and products developed. (Photo by Karin Gottschalk Marconi)

Marketing involves several areas of activity, among them the positioning and promoting of companies, products, brands, services, issues, and causes. The various strategies and techniques used by companies and organizations in the above examples demonstrate efforts to gain market share, loyal customers, and supporters by doing something that will be well regarded by the community. In every case, it would be fair to say that they stepped out from the pack and in some way tried to make a difference.

For their efforts, the marketplace continues to be a platform for imagination and innovation, and perhaps the world is a better place.

Ben & Jerry's may be as well known around the world for its support of environmental causes and social responsibility issues as it is for its rich-tasting, premium-priced ice cream. Despite its current ownership by a large global corporation, Ben & Jerry's remains true to its original mission to make the world a better place. (Photo by Karin Gottschalk Marconi)

S U M M A R Y

- In the past, the public may have been willing to accept the right thing being done for the wrong reason, but today's general public is more sophisticated and sees through efforts that are clearly self-serving.

- To have a hidden agenda and try to look good to the public while manipulating issues is a high-risk strategy that can easily backfire.

- A useful approach to avoid looking self-serving is to ensure that the beneficiary of the company's generosity issues public expressions of praise and gratitude. Otherwise, be open and direct in listing accomplishments, not coy in offering false humility or taking credit for the work of others.

- Generating public awareness of a program is critical. Being an anonymous benefactor is generous but nonproductive—and is certainly not marketing.

- A company's special occasion (an anniversary, a location opening, the founder's birthday) are ideal times to launch a commemorative cause marketing program.

- Heavily publicize the fact when a cause marketing program reaches its goal. Publicize it even more if the goal is exceeded.

- Taking on a cause that is bold and socially "heavy" when the company is not known for such things is a strong move.

- Use cause marketing as an opportunity to develop a constituency within the group of supporters of the cause.

- Explore ways the company's and nonprofit organization's vendors and affiliates can become involved in the causes.

- Keep the program fresh by adding new partners and new sites, such as an online component.

A Crash Course in Cause Marketing

When a company, an organization, an institution, or a nonprofit makes a decision committing itself to a cause marketing program, it can be a pivotal step in its future, potentially repositioning, redirecting, or redefining its focus and image. If taken seriously, the decision represents more than writing a check, lending its name, or sponsoring a fundraising effort. It means putting the reputation of all parties involved on one line, out front and at risk. If the head of a charity turns out to be dishonest, the company that has identified itself with that charity is subject to whatever fallout results. If the company is the subject of front-page (or even back-page) bad news, the image of a noble and worthy cause may be damaged, its ability to do good perhaps permanently impaired. What makes the effort worth pursuing is the sincere belief that something positive will result, the cause is right, people will be helped, awareness will be raised, and the public will remember and be inclined to reward those who had a role in making it happen.

Cause marketing is, at the start, about *believing*—in what is good and what is possible. The next steps are about making it happen. Whether the objective is a small local business helping to fund a local school athletic or music program, a large corporation committing itself to a literacy campaign or scholarship program, a sponsored campaign to benefit AIDS research or breast cancer

awareness or the elimination of world hunger or support for programs to help the homeless or save the environment—there are
enough challenges and people needing help that any entity with
even a modicum of social consciousness can find a place to focus
its efforts. Although some insist that God helps those who help
themselves, research referenced in this book alone confirms that
people respect, admire, and support those who choose to help
other people.

The principles of cause marketing are rooted in social responsibility, ethics, community service, and the belief that businesses can
do well by doing good. The rules, reasons, and rewards can be presented in concise terms. Take a deep breath and reread them as
often as needed:

- Research confirms that companies thought to be socially responsible are held in higher regard by their employees, customers, and the general public than are "nongiving" companies.
  Consequently, when given a choice, the public overwhelmingly
  chooses to do business with (and invest in) more socially responsible companies. Cause marketing works.

- It is important to *believe in your cause.* In an age of cynicism,
  many companies find their motives called into question when
  they take a position on behalf of a high-profile, worthy cause.
  Such companies are accused of acting out of self-interest
  rather than genuinely caring about helping others. To achieve
  maximum results from your cause marketing effort, believe in
  the cause you choose, offer a compelling case for your decision, and be totally committed, not simply "positioned" for the
  purpose of public relations. If the public believes in your
  cause, it will expect as much from you.

- A commitment to *corporate social responsibility, business ethics,
  values, vision,* and *the public interest* is the foundation of a good
  cause marketing effort.

- Well-managed companies conduct attitude and awareness research. It is important to know all that can be known (regardless of what you think you know) about the company, the cause, various nonprofit organizations concerned with the cause, competitors' positions, causes supported by competitors, and how the public feels about all of these. Knowledge is power . . . and research is a good idea.

- Have a plan. A cause marketing program is still a marketing program, and marketing programs need well-defined plans with a *situation analysis, objectives, strategy and tactics, a timeline, and a budget.*

- Understand your objectives. Philanthropy, contributions, donations, support funding, sponsorship, patronage, and advocacy are all much the same—only the amounts may vary. Cause marketing is a process in which the supporter of a cause or issue invests, expecting some acknowledgment of the support or other type of return on investment will be forthcoming, if only in goodwill from other supporters of a cause.

- Every public service ad is a form of cause marketing in that it is paid for by some individual, company, or organization advocating a position on the cause. Such sponsoring entities understand that one ad appearing one time is not likely to produce a good return on investment. Maximizing the visibility of such advertising is a function of marketing.

- Know all that you can know about specific regulatory and legal considerations relating to the cause and how such considerations may be different from state to state (as well as from country to country).

- Choose your partners carefully. Partners in cause marketing programs—usually a company and a nonprofit organization with a recognized commitment to the cause—must pursue their individual institutional objectives but must have a clear respect for each other and an understanding of each other's mission as well as their joint agreements.

- Cause marketing partners must understand each other's needs, capabilities, resources, and cultures. Misunderstanding is often more damaging than mistrust.

- Written agreements between partners ensure clarity about expectations, responsibilities, rights, ownership, and obligations. Business for Social Responsibility (BSR) recommends getting the deal in writing. Even though several of the most successful cause marketing partnerships have operated under the most informal of agreements—sometimes little more than a handshake—such an arrangement can be very risky and very costly should a misunderstanding arise, particularly about areas of responsibility and finances. Even written agreements are only as good as the degree to which people understand them and trust each other. People in organizations come and go for any number of reasons, but a clear and concise Statement of Purpose with an allocation of responsibility lasts through campaigns and generations.

- Some very explicit written agreements, like many marketing plans, are long, written in legalese, and overly specific . . . and usually no one reads them except the lawyers who write them. *Clear, brief, concise* agreements are better than long, detailed formal agreements that go unread. It is often said that the first time some people read the contracts they've signed is before going to court after being sued for not adhering to the contract. Even informal agreements are better when written and understood.

- A well-crafted outline for a cause marketing campaign should appeal to a specific target audience without excluding others who may at some point become part of the audience. Clearly

wear jeans for life
a life **free** of breast cancer

Lee National Denim Day®
october 5, 2001
We Fit Your Life.   ©2001 Lee Apparel

Actress Lucy Liu learned from her own experience with early detection that breast cancer awareness saves lives. Join Lucy in her effort to promote breast cancer education and work towards a cure by participating in Lee National Denim Day™. Donate $5 to the Susan G. Komen Foundation and wear jeans to work on October 5, 2001. Ask your event coordinator for details.

"Lee National Denim Day" put the company name on a day and focused attention on its product while asking for $5 donations, 100 percent of which would be sent to the Susan G. Komen Breast Cancer Foundation to fund research. The presence of actress Lucy Liu in ads for the program helped to get attention. Lee's choice of a cause to support helps further move its brand image away from what was once that of a rugged male-oriented product. When a company can change how people perceive its product through an association with a cause, it's smart marketing. (Copyright 2001 Lee Apparel) outline the benefits to the company, the organization, and the public so everyone knows why this is a good plan.

- Cause marketing partners should have an appreciation for each other's goals and objectives and be comfortable working together. Partnerships that don't feel right usually aren't.

- Partners in a cause marketing effort should be flexible but still have a clear understanding of who will do what, when, and under what limitations.

- Support for a cause comes from the inside in two respects. First, support comes from a sense of personal belief and commitment and, second, from inside the company or organization. Your own people need to be invited to participate, kept informed, and be unqualified supporters of the program; otherwise, it is being built on a soft foundation.

- Clearly define the creative aspect of the program and its benefits to all stakeholders and constituents.

- Have a clear understanding of potential risks to reputations and resources.

- Know the expected minimum guarantees; have both an expiration date or an exit strategy if the program's not working and a provision for extending or expanding in case the program should exceed expectations.

- Encourage volunteers, both inside and outside the company and nonprofit organization, and treat them with respect and generosity. Their contributions can be invaluable. Keep them on your side and motivated.

- Use the media to help carry your message—print, television, radio, direct mail, out-of-home (billboards, transit posters), and the Internet—but rely on professional expertise. All of the media may reach the same people, but each has different requirements, deadlines, potential risks, and costs.

- Crisis management is part of modern marketing. Just as a cause has its supporters, virtually every cause has its detractors or those who disagree with its mission. Know as much as you can about critics, adversaries, special interest groups, and potential downside risks; in addition, have a plan to respond to worst-case scenarios.

- Don't necessarily expect fairness or objectivity from the media or the marketplace. It's a cynical and sad commentary, but too many diverse factors and entities operating with their own agenda require you to keep up your guard.

- Strive to create a *reservoir of goodwill* from which you can draw in times of crisis. Publicize good works and don't let the first news the public reads, hears, or sees about you be bad news.

- Be honest, be positive, and, if bad news happens, tell your side of the story first if possible. That helps define and control the news and avoids your appearing defensive.

- The public will forgive companies and organizations that make mistakes if they take charge after a problem occurs and assume responsibility. Be honest and always offer as complete an account of a situation as may be needed.

- Always try to present bad news in a larger context than a current problem, so it becomes only one part of the company's, organization's, or cause's story, not the whole story. Be honest and believable in your version of events. Some companies have embellished or exaggerated facts beyond reasonable plausibility.

- Don't take long-time supporters for granted. Give the public clear reasons to be on your side in both good times and bad.

- Crises often create opportunities. In bad times, explore ways to position the company, organization, or cause to emerge in a more positive way. It is possible to leave even your harshest critics believing that you acted honorably and did the right things.

- Guard against overreaching and overreacting to both positive and negative situations.

- Get help. Experienced and skilled professionals offer counsel in marketing, PR, and crisis management. Don't be afraid to bring in competent, objective experts in times of great stress and difficulty.

- Don't "showboat." Take credit for good work but exercise humility. The public likes and admires strength but finds arrogance contemptible.

- Position your subject as socially responsible before it is necessary to.

- Be direct. Companies discovered to have a hidden agenda lose the confidence of the public and invite suspicion in the future.

- Maintain a steady flow of publicity activity rather than laying low until you have a "big" announcement. People like what is familiar, so keep yourself visible and in front of the public to achieve a greater level of recognition, awareness, and support.

- Special occasions are reasons for an event or announcement worthy of media coverage. Share your experiences with your public. Knowing a company has been around for 25 years or is under new management or has been run by the same family for several generations tells a story that promotes familiarity. The public is interested in knowing more about people and things with which it is already familiar—such as what cause the company supports that encourages the public to like it even more.

■ A cause marketing partnership should benefit the company, the cause and its nonprofit organization, and ultimately, of course, the people or subject the effort was intended to help. In theory, everyone wins. In real life, however, theories have been known to hit snags. A solid plan, a written agreement, a clear understanding, and commitment by all sides minimize the likelihood of glitches in the theory turning into crises.

Cause marketing seems to be a simple concept, yet it continues to be a subject of controversy. Given the intensity of debate within families and communities over candidates, sports teams, hairstyles, and musical tastes, the existence of disagreement over support for issues or a cause should not surprise anyone. But marketers and others responsible for winning approval and affirmation from the public are not just anyone.

As the cost of doing business continues to rise, alternatives seem to be more plentiful, and competition grows even more intense. The challenge of being the name, company, or brand of choice becomes even greater. Cause marketing provides opportunities to become recognized by new constituencies loyal to specific issues and efforts. At the same time, cause marketing positions a business to win a committed share of the market and at the same time contribute to making life better for people in need or the world in general.

Throughout the world's history, natural disasters or other catastrophic events have served as catalysts to bring people together— to move those who can to contribute help and resources without hesitation or reservation—and to put humanity and social responsibility ahead of profits. Many companies and individuals come forward and do their part and more, while people, the community, and the media see it and remember. Being part of a good cause without hesitating to consider its short-term cost is reactive.

Cause marketing doesn't wait for the next dark day to provide a reason to come forward. And smart marketing involves taking advantage of opportunities, creating opportunities, and making the most of every minute . . . starting now.

BIBLIOGRAPHY

Alsop, Ronald. "Perils of Corporate Philanthropy." *Wall Street Journal*, 16 January 2002.

Brown, Tom. "Assessing Corporate Social Responsibility." *Harvard Management Update*, April 2001.

Business for Social Responsibility Education Fund. *Cause-Related Marketing: Partnership Guidelines & Case Studies*. 2001.

Council on Economic Priorities. *The Corporate Report Card*. New York: Dutton, published by Penguin Group, 1998.

Drucker, Peter. "What Business Can Learn from Nonprofits." *Harvard Business Review* 67, no. 4 (1989).

Earle, Richard. *The Art of Cause Marketing*. Chicago: NTC/McGraw Hill, 2000.

Galbraith, John Kenneth. *The Affluent Society*. 3d ed. Boston: Houghton Mifflin, 1976.

Helperin, Joanna R. "All for the Cause." <Business2.com> 24 October 2000.

Johnson, Steve. "Patriotism for Sale." *Chicago Tribune*, 18 October 2001.

Larsen, Jennifer. "Partnerships Teaching at Field Park." *Doings Newspapers*, 10 January 2002.

Lieberman, David. "Corporations put aside egos, rivalry to help out." *USA Today*, 19 October 2001.

Marconi, Joe. "Marketing after 9/11." *Interface*, American Marketing Association, (Chicago), November-December 2001.

———. *Crisis Marketing: When Good Things Happen to Good Companies*. Chicago: NTC/McGraw-Hill, 1997.

Martin, Douglas. "Dave Thomas, 64, Wendy's Founder Dies." *New York Times*, 9 January 2002.

O'Neil, John. "Charities Get a Big Helping of Uncertainty." *New York Times*, 12 November 2001.

Osbourne, David, and Ted Gaebler. *Reinventing Government*. New York: Plume, 1992.

Sagawa, Shirley, and Eli Segal. *Common Interest, Common Good.* Boston: Harvard Business School Press, 2000.

Weeden, Curt. *Corporate Social Investing.* San Francisco: Berrett-Koehler, 1998.

ABOUT BUSINESS FOR SOCIAL RESPONSIBILITY

Business for Social Responsibility (BSR) is a global nonprofit organization that helps member companies achieve commercial success in ways that respect ethical values, people, communities, and the environment. Advancing the adoption of business practices that build a more just and sustainable world, BSR provides information, tools, and advisory services to make corporate social responsibility an integral part of business operations and strategies. BSR also promotes private, public, and independent sector collaborations and contributes to global efforts to advance the field of corporate social responsibility. BSR member companies have nearly $2 trillion in combined annual revenues and employ more than six million workers around the world. For more information, visit <www.bsr.org>.

CAUSE MARKETING WORKS WHEN YOUR WHOLE TEAM IS INVOLVED!

For quantities of *Cause Marketing: Build Your Image and Bottom Line through Socially Responsible Partnerships, Programs, and Events,* please contact Terri Joseph in Special Sales at 800-621-9621, extension 4307, or by e-mail at tjoseph@dearborn.com.

Your company also can order this book with a customized cover featuring your name, logo, and message.

Dearborn™
Trade Publishing
A **Kaplan Professional** Company